MW01626184

Mantle

Windy Day in August, at Nauvoo

Mantle

Windy Day in August, at Nauvoo

When the Mantle of the
Prophet Joseph Smith Fell on Brigham Young,
and He Was Sustained as Leader of the Church According
to the Doctrine of Apostolic Succession

by
Robert G. Mouritsen

Mantle—Windy Day in August, at Nauvoo

Westheather Development Company

Distributed by

Book Design and Layout by Tom Child Design

ISBN: 0-9748385-0-0
Library of Congress Control Number:

First Printing, August 2004

Printed in the United States of America

10 9 8 7 6 5 4 3 2 1

"In the afternoon, according to my request, the people assembled by thousands. I laid before them the order of the Church and the power of the Priesthood. After a long and laborious talk of about two hours in the open air with the wind blowing, the Church was of one heart and one mind."

(From *The Diary of Brigham Young, Thursday, August 8, 1844.*)

"Someone has said . . . and I believe it to be absolutely true: '*That person is not truly converted until he sees the power of God resting upon the leaders of this church, and it goes down into his heart like fire.*' Until the members . . . have that conviction that . . . these men of God . . . have been properly appointed by the hand of God, they are not truly converted."

(President Harold B. Lee, *"Faith in Leadership,"* from an address at the General Priesthood Meeting, Saturday, April 8, 1972, cited in *Conference Report*, April 1972, p. 118, italics added.)

To the memory of my father,
Glendale Mouritsen, and my mother,
Jean Brockbank Mouritsen, who,
in their lives, saw the power of God
resting upon the
leaders of the Church

Table of Contents

An Opening Comment

The original draft of this work was prepared thirty years ago, in August, 1974, under the title *Windy Day in August, at Nauvoo,* and a version without the Addendum was circulated. In 1977, the manuscript was modified to include reference to an address presented by Elder William Grant Bangerter in the October General Conference that year. Subsequently, as many friends, and associates who have been acquainted with the author in a variety of settings, have become aware of the study, the author has responded to numerous requests for copies.

In 1992, the author's brother, Dale C. Mouritsen, Director of the Cupertino Institute and an institute instructor in California for many years, and Ronald O. Barney, Senior Archivist at the Church Archives in Salt Lake City and an associate of the author in Church service for many years, urged that the work be published. Ron Barney kindly furnished the testimony of his great-great-grandfather. For the encouragement and helpful suggestions of these two good men, I am very grateful.

The writer had hoped to publish the work in conjunction with the 150th anniversary of the event in 1994 but care for a special son, demands of profession and Church service made that impossible. In 1995, the original was dusted off, recast under the same title, and presented as an address in a conference of the Kaysville Utah Crestwood Stake, on Saturday, September 4, 1995.

This is not a work of fiction. The author has felt that the story of the restoration, from accounts of the events which brought the family of Joseph and Lucy Smith from Vermont to western New York, to accounts of the organization of the most recent Stake in the burgeoning world-wide Church, is a spellbinding story and can stand on its own merits. There was "faith in every footstep" and "miracles on every page." The story begins with the appearance of the Father and the Son to the boy Joseph in the spring of 1820. It continues, as the Prophet said, "through all the travels and tribulations of this Church of Jesus Christ of Latter-day Saints," to events surrounding acquisition of land for the newest Temple.

Whenever the accounts which comprise this saga are presented, with such detail as may be drawn from histories, sermons, journals and diaries—accounts of eyewitnesses, it is an amazing, powerful story. There is a simple reason for this: God's hand has guided the restoration, from the beginning to the present day. When any aspect of the story is told, as it occurred, with no embellishment and without apology, the hand of God is revealed and there will be the witness of the Spirit. The truth is far more powerful than fiction.

Down through the years, the author has greatly respected Milton V. Backman, Jr., Larry C. Porter, Robert J. Matthews,

Calvin P. Rudd, C. Wilford Griggs and many others who are or have served as professors or instructors. Whenever the Saints are privileged to sit at the feet of one who knows, someone who has "walked the ground," the story has great power. When the Saints can read true accounts of Mormon history, or listen to someone, who has poured over the available records with an eye of faith and is able to describe events of the restoration as they actually occurred, the story has great power.

This book tells the story of an important aspect of the restoration. It is a glimpse into that momentous week when the mantle of the Prophet Joseph Smith fell upon Brigham Young. It is an account that is based upon the records of Brigham Young and Wilford Woodruff who were Apostles at the time and later became Presidents of the Church, Willard Richards who was an Apostle at the time and had been with the Prophet and Hyrum in Carthage Jail, Thomas Bullock, George Laub, William Clayton and others who served at various times as scribes and recorders to the Prophet. The work is also based on the testimony of numerous diarists, humble Saints who were present and witnessed the event, and then wrote about it in diaries, letters or personal histories. Although many references to the event could be cited, the writer felt in 1974, and still feels, that an exhaustive catalogue of statements might make the account tedious, and that the sampling presented here is sufficient to constitute a witness.

Foundation Witness

After the martyrdom of the Prophet Joseph Smith and his brother Hyrum, there was confusion about who should lead the Church. In that uncertain period of July and early August, before the Twelve Apostles could assemble in Nauvoo and be sustained, with Brigham Young at their head, the Saints were, President Wilford Woodruff observed, "as sheep without a shepherd." Sister Mary Ann Sterns Winters, a girl of only eleven that fateful summer, recalled, "oh, the horror and gloom and heartaches and trials of those days. The very atmosphere was so oppressive that it seemed difficult to breathe. Everything seemed to stand still . . . the headlight was obscured and the darkness was profound."

Upon his arrival in Nauvoo in early August, Sidney Rigdon called for the Saints to assemble on the morning of Thursday, August 8, in a "prayer meeting" at the Stand, where he intended to have himself sustained as "guardian of the Church." After Brigham Young arrived in Nauvoo, the evening of Tuesday, August 6, and a majority of the Twelve could be assembled, it was determined that a formal assembly of the Saints should be convened on Tuesday, August 13. But before the close of the "prayer meeting" on the 8th, out of "compassion" for the Saints and to blunt the confusion fostered by the posturing of Sidney Rigdon, a decision was made to move the formal assembly forward from the 13th to the 8th—that very afternoon. It was when Brigham Young arose at the close of the morning "prayer meeting" to announce this change, that the "mantle of the Prophet" rested upon him so that to the Saints he had the voice, the gestures, even the very appearance of the Prophet Joseph Smith. Immediately the gloom was dispelled. The Saints felt that they had "heard the voice of the shepherd at last."

Those willing to discredit testimonies that the mantle of the Prophet fell upon Brigham Young point to confusion in the histories as to when the actual meeting occurred. They cite confusion in the various diaries at which meeting the event occurred, and differences in the descriptions of those who were witnesses to the matter. They worry about the lapse of years, sometimes many years, between the meeting in 1844 and when the witnesses wrote about the meeting in their histories, or presented their testimonies in public discourses, or dictated accounts of their experience to others. Some who address the subject cite selected journal entries of the event, showing that the diary entries disagree on some minor points, then announce their "findings" that there is "conflict" in the eyewitness accounts. They invoke terms, such as "enthusiastic," "emotional," "overzealous," or even "desperate," to dismiss accounts or the recollections by the early Church members of this event.

The reasons that members and even a few early historians made mistakes about the day are not difficult to assess. There was a meeting of Brigham Young, others of the Twelve, and several leaders of the Church, including William Marks, then President of the Nauvoo Stake, and Sidney Rigdon, which convened at the Seventies Hall on Wednesday, August 7. There was the "prayer meeting" called by Sidney Rigdon and convened on Thursday morning, August 8th. There was the proposal of a formal assembly of Priesthood quorums and members, called on a motion presented by Brigham Young and sustained by priesthood leaders in the meeting at the Seventies Hall, to convene on Tuesday, August 13th. (This formal assembly of Priesthood quorums and members, originally called for Tuesday, August 13th, was, by the decision of Brigham Young and perhaps the Twelve, made in the late morning of August 8th, moved forward to the afternoon of August 8th). And there were all of the formal sessions of the 14th Semi-annual General Conference of the Church, convened in Nauvoo just a few months later, on Sunday, Monday and Tuesday, October 6th, 7th and 8th, 1844, which sustained the Twelve with Brigham Young at their head to lead the Church.

All of this occurred within the 100 days between the Martyrdom in June and the General Conference in October. These were days marked by fear and anxiety, confusion, posturing by ambitious pretenders, a final settlement of questions of leadership, restructuring, filling vacancies in the quorums of leadership, focus on completing the temple, plans to abandon Nauvoo, and preparations for the trek west. The wonder is not that some of the Saints, witness to the events which are the subject of this study, might err in their account of when the meetings convened, or at which meeting the witness of the mantle was poured out upon the Church, but that they had the presence of mind to record or recall the matter at all.

But in their assessments, perhaps without intent, critics foster questions about a fundamental fact of the Restoration, that the authority conferred by Holy Angels upon the Prophet Joseph Smith continued with the Church after his death, and continues today. Those who criticize do face a daunting task, however, for the larger issue in dealing with this meeting, when the mantle of the Prophet Joseph Smith fell upon Brigham Young, is that thousands of people were there, and hundreds of them recorded their witness of the event.

I have felt that a written account of this remarkable event would be of value. I have attempted to show from the sources what actually occurred in the changing of the meeting date from Tuesday, August 13, 1844, to Thursday afternoon, August 8, 1844, present a sampling of the remarkable harmony in the diary accounts, and note the integrity in the story as details of the various diary accounts are brought together.

Here, in the account of this miraculous transformation, we find one of the foundation testimonies of the Restoration, a principle that must be believed if the Church is true. We have the testimony of the Prophet Joseph himself, of the restoration by Holy Angels to him of all the keys, powers and truths of all the dispensations,[1] a testimony that, together with his brother Hyrum, he sealed with his blood. We have the testimony of the

1. D&C 128:18–21.

Three Witnesses to the Book of Mormon; and then the testimony of the Eight Witnesses, certifying as to the divine origin of that record which contains the fulness of the gospel. We have the accounts of the early Saints who participated in the Pentecostal events of March, 1836, when the Kirtland Temple was dedicated and the sacred sealing keys were restored. But of what value are keys and powers and eternal truths if they are lost by the Martyrdom of the Prophet Joseph Smith? Could they be lost? Were they lost? Nothing that we do in the Church has any validity, no eternal significance, if the keys were lost.

So then we have this testimony, the testimony of the hundreds of Saints who witnessed the very fact of the Mantle of the Prophet Joseph Smith falling upon Brigham Young. It was assurance from a heavenly source, poured out upon an assembly of the Saints sufficient in number that their collective testimony could not then, and cannot now, be ignored, conferring a divine witness, a reassurance that ranks with all the other foundation testimonies of the Restoration, that the keys and powers and truths were not lost, but continue in the Church.

And it is a powerful testimony. Hundreds testified of the transformation of Brigham Young before their very eyes—some recorded that they heard the voice of Joseph, some felt that they saw Joseph, and some that the person who addressed them that morning had the voice, the gestures, and even the very appearance of the Prophet Joseph Smith himself. The testimony is made all the more powerful by the fact that the people were standing or seated with their backs toward the Stand, away from where Brigham Young was sitting during the discourse of Sidney Rigdon. Then, when Sidney Rigdon finished his discourse and sat down, they heard the voice of the Prophet Joseph Smith behind them, and rising to their feet, and turning around, they saw resting upon Brigham the very mantle of Joseph Smith. Witness of divine things may vary from person to person, depending upon faith, obedience, preparation, trustworthiness and capacity to receive. Some of these people testified that they heard the voice of Joseph, some described the gestures of Joseph, and indeed some saw the very appearance of Joseph. And thus there was established the witness, not of one but of thousands, that the authority and keys held by Joseph Smith ***could be*** passed to others, that the authority and keys ***were*** passed to others, and continue today.

Robert G. Mouritsen
Sunday, August 8, 2004
Kaysville, Utah

Mantle

Windy Day in August, at Nauvoo

Precedents—The Mantle is Handed Down

After "Moses the servant of the Lord" was taken away,[2] Joshua, the son of Nun, succeeded him. It was written that "Joshua . . . was full of the spirit of wisdom; for Moses had laid his hands upon him: and the children of Israel hearkened unto him, and did as the Lord commanded . . ."[3] And "the Lord spake unto Joshua . . . Moses' minister saying, Moses my servant is dead; now therefore arise . . .

> *"There shall not any man be able to stand before thee all the days of thy life: as I was with Moses, so I will be with thee: I will not fail thee, nor forsake thee . . .*
>
> *"Only be thou strong and very courageous, that thou mayest observe to do according to all the law, which Moses my servant commanded thee: turn not from it to the right hand or to the left, that thou mayest prosper whithersoever thou goest . . .*
>
> *"Have not I commanded thee? Be strong and of a good courage; be not afraid, neither be thou dismayed: for the Lord thy God is with thee whithersoever thou goest."*[4]

There is a similar account in scripture, when the mantle of the Prophet Elijah was passed to Elisha. According to the record, Elijah, with Elisha standing by him—fearful that Elijah

2. Joshua 1:1; Alma 45:19.
3. Deuteronomy 34:9.
4. Joshua 1:2–9.

might be taken away from him and therefore unwilling to leave his side, "stood by the River Jordan.

"And Elijah took his mantle . . . and smote the waters, and they were divided hither and thither, so that they two went over on dry ground.

"And it came to pass, when they were gone over, that Elijah said unto Elisha, Ask what I shall do for thee, before I be taken away from thee. And Elisha said, I pray thee, let a double portion of thy spirit be upon me.

"And he said, Thou hast asked a hard thing: never-the-less, if thou see me when I am taken from thee, it shall be so unto thee; but if not, it shall not be so.

"And it came to pass, as they still went on, and talked, that, behold, there appeared a chariot of fire, and horses of fire, and parted them both asunder; and Elijah went up by a whirlwind into heaven.

"And Elisha . . . cried, My father, my father . . . And he saw him no more: and he took hold of his own clothes, and rent them in two pieces.

"**He took up also the mantle of Elijah that fell from him**, *and went back, and stood by the bank of Jordan;*

"And he . . . smote the waters, and said, Where is the Lord God of Elijah? and when he also had smitten the waters, they parted hither and thither: and Elisha went over.

"And when the sons of the prophets . . . at Jericho saw him, they said, The spirit of Elijah doth rest on Elisha. And they came to meet him, and bowed themselves to the ground before him."[5]

---

5. 2 Kings 2:7–15, italics added.

In this final age of the world, the mantle has been restored to the earth for "the last time,"[6] and will be handed down from one Prophet to another until "He reigns whose right it is to reign."[7] President Spencer W. Kimball, eleventh in succession from the Prophet Joseph, testified: "the work goes forward—and one prophet succeeds another . . .

> *". . . the mantle of Joseph Smith fell on Brigham Young when he seemed to be transformed before the people who seemed to hear the voice of Joseph and see the person of Joseph. This remarkable miracle was attested to by great numbers of people. The mantle of Joseph fell from Brigham to John Taylor, to Wilford Woodruff, to Lorenzo Snow, to Joseph F. Smith, to Heber J. Grant, to George Albert Smith . . ."*[8]

And so on, to David O. McKay, to Joseph Fielding Smith, to Harold B. Lee, to Spencer W. Kimball, to Ezra Taft Benson, to Howard W. Hunter, and to Gordon B. Hinckley, the great Prophet of our day. But the order of Apostolic Succession by which this transfer occurs, of handing down the mantle so that each successor has authority to excercise the fulness of keys and powers they receive when they are first ordained Apostles, first had to be tested, and that test is the subject of this writing.

---

6. D&C 112:30.

7. D&C 58:22. Compare D&C 136:37.

8. President Spencer W. Kimball, *"Revelations Ancient and Modern,"* from an address that was presented in the Friday afternoon general session of the 136th Semi-annual General Conference, in the Tabernacle in Salt Lake City, Friday, September 30, 1996, as cited in ***Conference Report***, October 1966, p. 25.

The Prophet Established the Doctrines of Succession

While he was alive, in the course of his ministry, the Prophet Joseph Smith established two orders of succession in the Church:[9] first, in the earliest years of the Restoration, the order of Associate President Succession,[10] and then later, as the Restoration moved forward and the Quorum of the Twelve Apostles was organized and gained experience, the order of Apostolic Succession.

Under the protocols of Associate President Succession, the First Presidency would include an Associate President who would be ranked second only to the President, whose authority, knowledge and personal witness would be comparable if not identical to that of the President,[11] and who, in the Prophet's

---

9. Robert G. Mouritsen, *"Establishment of Associate President Succession," **The Office of Associate President of The Church of Jesus Christ of Latter-day Saints*** (Master's thesis, Brigham Young University, 1972), pp. 128–135.

10. The office was first designated as "Assistant President," (Manuscript History of The Church of Jesus Christ of Latter-day Saints [Historical Department, Salt Lake City], Book A, p. 1), but both men who held the office, Oliver Cowdery and Hyrum Smith, were described as holding the same keys and authority that the Prophet himself held, and therefore "Associate President" is a more accurate term. An "Assistant President" would hold a position subordinate to the President, but an "Associate President" would hold a position or rank more nearly equal with that of the President. President Joseph Fielding Smith, in his last published reference to the office, used the term "Associate President" with emphasis, and even changed the reference from "Assistant" to "Associate" in his quotations from the Manuscript History.

11. Oliver Cowdery was the first to hold the office of Associate President, and when he was no longer worthy of the office, Hyrum Smith was appointed to hold the office in his stead, to "act in concert also with my servant Joseph," and to receive the "keys . . . and priesthood, and gifts of the priesthood that once were put upon him that was my servant Oliver Cowdery." (D&C 124:95). Of this, President Joseph Fielding Smith has written that "by revelation through Joseph Smith, Hyrum was called and ordained to the priesthood and standing once held by Oliver Cowdery" and "the Lord said" of Hyrum:

language, would "preside in the absence of the President."[12] In the event of the President's death, such a First Presidency would not dissolve, but would remain intact and continue to function under the leadership of the Associate President.[13]

"And from this time forth I appoint unto him that he may be a prophet, and a seer, and a revelator unto my church, as well as my servant Joseph;

"That he may act in concert also with my servant Joseph; and that he shall receive counsel from my servant Joseph, who shall show unto him the keys whereby he may ask and receive, and be crowned with the same blessing, and glory, and honor, and priesthood, and gifts of the priesthood, that once were put upon him that was my servant Oliver Cowdery;

"That my servant Hyrum may bear record of the things which I shall show unto him, that his name may be had in honorable remembrance from generation to generation, forever and ever" (D&C 124:94–96).

"In accord with this calling and commandment, the *Prophet Joseph Smith conferred upon Hyrum Smith all the keys, authority and gifts of the priesthood which he, the Prophet, held,* and which were formerly held by Oliver Cowdery. The Lord also revealed to Hyrum Smith all that was necessary to make him *completely and to the full degree, a witness with his brother Joseph,* as a prophet, seer, revelator and president of the Church, and to stand through all time and all eternity at the head of this dispensation with his brother Joseph, a witness for Jesus Christ.

"Thus, we see, Hyrum Smith became a President of the Church with Joseph Smith, which place Oliver Cowdery might have held had he not wavered and fallen from his exalted station . . .

"Oliver Cowdery turned away and lost his place, and he ceased . . . as far as the priesthood was concerned, to be the 'Second Elder,' the 'Second President' . . .

"It went on in that way—Joseph . . . President, Sidney Rigdon and Hyrum . . . counselors—until the 19th day of January, 1841. On that day the Lord commanded Joseph . . . to ordain Hyrum . . . and confer upon him all the keys, authority, and privileges [that were once] placed upon the head of Oliver Cowdery, and make him the 'Second President' of the Church. Hyrum Smith, like Oliver Cowdery, has not received his place properly in the minds of many as the 'Second President' of the Church—but that was his place." (President Joseph Fielding Smith, *"Joint Witnesses," **Doctrines of Salvation***, Compiled and Edited by Elder Bruce R. McConkie, 3 Volumes, 24th Printing [Salt Lake City: Bookcraft, Inc., 1990]. Vol. 1, pp. 217–222, italic added).

12. Manuscript History, Book A, p. 1.

13. Ibid. Compare Mouritsen, ***The Office of Associate President***, p. 131, and

Apostolic Succession was provided to operate in situations where there was no Associate President, whereupon, at the death of the President, the First Presidency would be entirely dissolved. Leadership of the Church would fall upon the Quorum of the Twelve, the body upon whose members the Prophet had conferred all the keys he himself held,[14] with their

---

Joseph Smith, ***History of The Church of Jesus Christ of Latter-day Saints***, Compiled and Edited by B. H. Roberts, 7 Volumes, 2nd Printing (Salt Lake City: Deseret Book Company, 1978), Vol. 2, p. 374.

14. Elder Orson Hyde, one of the Twelve, testified that "before I went east on the 4th of April last [1844], we were in council with Brother Joseph almost every day for weeks. Says Brother Joseph in one of those councils, 'there is something going to happen; I don't know what it is, but the Lord bids me to hasten and give you your endowment before the temple is finished.' He conducted us through every ordinance of the holy priesthood, and when he had gone through with all the ordinances he rejoiced very much, and says, 'now if they kill me you have got all the keys, and all the ordinances and you can confer them upon others, and the hosts of Satan will not be able to tear down the kingdom, as fast as you will be able to build it up; and now,' says he, 'on your shoulders will the responsibility of leading this people rest, for the Lord is going to let me rest a while.' ***Now why did he say to the Twelve, 'on your shoulders will this responsibility rest,' why did he not mention Brother Hyrum? The spirit knew that Hyrum would be taken with him, and hence he did not mention his name; Elder Rigdon's name was not mentioned,*** although he was here all the time, but he did not attend our councils." (From Minutes of a meeting held at the Stand in Nauvoo, Sunday, September 8, 1844, the ***Times and Seasons***, 6 Volumes, Exact Lithographic Reprint of Original Edition [Zwickau, Germany: F. Ullmann KG, 1967] Vol. 5, p. 651, italic added).

In 1844, Wilford Woodruff addressed the question of Elder Sidney Rigdon's claims in a letter to the ***Times and Seasons***, in which he testified that "a few months before his death," the "Prophet . . . organized the Quorum of the Twelve . . . to prepare them for the endowment. And when they had received their endowment, and actually received the keys of the Kingdom of God, and oracles of God, keys of revelation and the pattern of heavenly things," the Prophet "exclaimed, 'upon your shoulders the Kingdom rests, and you must round up your shoulders, and bear it; for I have had to do it until now.'" (***Times and Seasons***, Vol. 6, p. 698). In 1897, President Wilford Woodruff testified that "in the early spring of 1844 in Nauvoo, the Prophet Joseph Smith called the Twelve Apostles together and he delivered unto them the ordinances

President at the head.[15] Apostolic Succession was also provided to operate in situations where there was an Associate President, but if the death of the Associate President occurred at the same time, or just prior to the death of the President, then again, the First Presidency would be entirely dissolved and leadership of the Church would fall upon the Quorum of the Twelve Apostles.

The Prophet Joseph instituted both orders of succession prior to his death, and explained them to Brigham Young, to members of the Quorum of the Twelve, and to others. The Prophet also communicated the clear sense that Associate President succession held precedence.[16]

---

of the Church and Kingdom of God; and all of the keys and powers that God had bestowed upon him, he sealed upon our heads. He told us we must round up our shoulders and bear off this kingdom or we would be damned. I am the only man now living in the flesh who heard that testimony from his mouth, and I know it is true by the power of God manifest through him. At that meeting, he began to speak about three hours upon the subject of the Kingdom. His face was clear as amber, and he was covered with a power that I have never seen in the flesh before." ("*Remarkable Testimony of President Wilford Woodruff,*" ***The New Era***, Vol. 2 [January 1972], p. 66).

15. The doctrine and the protocols that govern Apostolic Succession are set forth in "*Selecting, Sustaining, Ordaining and Setting Apart a New President of the Church,*" ***The Improvement Era*** (Salt Lake City: The Church of Jesus Christ of Latter-day Saints, 1897–1970), July, 1956, Vol. 59, p. 528.

16. President Joseph Fielding Smith explained: "President Brigham Young, after the death of Joseph Smith, when they were discussing the matter of succession, said: 'Did Joseph Smith ordain a successor? He did. Who was it? It was Hyrum. But Hyrum fell martyr before the Prophet did.'[see statement by President Brigham Young, ***Times and Seasons***, Vol. 5, p. 683–684] . . . if Hyrum Smith had hearkened to the Prophet and taken his family to Cincinnati, ***there would have been a President of the Church and it would not have been Brigham Young***. Brigham Young was President of the Council of the Twelve, and Hyrum Smith would have been President of the Church by virtue of his ordination, holding the place held by Oliver Cowdery.

"That is as plain and simple as it can be, as it is stated in our scriptures and in the history of the Church. Joseph Smith and Hyrum Smith, after 1841, signed documents

Hyrum Smith was called by revelation and ordained to the office of Associate President on Sunday, January 24, 1841.[17] He served faithfully, and occupied that high office when he was killed in June, 1844. Brigham Young and others of the Twelve clearly understood that had Hyrum survived the Prophet Joseph, that is, had Hyrum not been slain at Carthage Jail that fateful Thursday, June 27, 1844,[18] he would have presided over the Church according to the order of Associate President Succession. As the President of the Church, Hyrum could have

---

as Presidents of the Church. With many members of the Church Hyrum Smith was just the Patriarch. Hyrum Smith received a double portion. He received the office of Patriarch which belonged to his father and came to him by right, and also received the keys to be 'Second President' and precede the counselors as Oliver Cowdery had done. So he would have remained as President of the Church had he not died a martyr." (Smith, *"Joseph and Hyrum Joint Presidents of Church, Order of Succession in Presidency,"* ***Doctrines of Salvation,*** Vol. 1, pp. 217–222).

17. See D&C 124:94–96. Compare Smith, *"Reconstruction of Church Affairs at Nauvoo,"* ***History of the Church,*** Vol. 4, pp. 274–286.

18. President Joseph Fielding Smith explained: "But here is another point. He had to die. Why? Because we read in the scriptures that the testimony is not of force without the death of the testator—that is, in his particular case, and in the case of Christ. It was just as necessary that Hyrum Smith lay down his life a martyr for this cause as a witness for God as it was for Joseph Smith, so the Lord permitted them both to be taken in that way and both sealed their testimony with their blood. Both of them held the keys of the dispensation of the fulness of times jointly, and they will through all the ages of eternity. Then naturally the Council of the Twelve came into its place, and by right Brigham Young became President of the Church.

"Had Oliver Cowdery remained true, had he been faithful to his testimony and his calling as the 'Second Elder' and Assistant President of the Church, I am just as satisfied as I am that I am here that Oliver Cowdery would have gone to Carthage with the Prophet Joseph Smith and laid down his life instead of Hyrum Smith. That would have been his right. Maybe it sounds a little strange to speak of martyrdom as being a right, but it was a right. Oliver Cowdery lost it and Hyrum Smith received it. According to the law of witnesses—and this is a divine law—it had to be." (Smith, *"The Divine Law of Witnesses—No Assistant* [Associate] *President Needed Today,"* ***Doctrines of Salvation,*** Vol. 1, pp. 217–222.)

used his brother's Counselors or called two others to stand with him to constitute the continuing First Presidency.[19]

Hyrum's Death Brought Apostolic Succession to the Fore

But under the hail of assassins' bullets at the Carthage jail, Hyrum fell a martyr before Joseph did.[20] Thus, at the death of the Prophet Joseph Smith, there was no surviving Associate President to continue that First Presidency.[21] Consequently that First Presidency was dissolved[22] and the order of Apostolic Succession was in full force and effect. Brigham Young was

---

19. President Joseph Fielding Smith, in *"Foreword,"* Pearson Corbett, ***Hyrum Smith: Patriarch*** (Salt Lake City: Deseret Book Company, 1963), pp. xii–xvi. See note #16 above.

20. Smith, *"Close of the Prophet—A Journal Narrative of the Prophet's Life, The Assault On the Prison—Martyrdom of Joseph And Hyrum,"* ***History of the Church***, Vol. 6, pp. 546, 617–618.

21. President Joseph Fielding Smith noted that "the question is sometimes asked: If Oliver Cowdery was ordained to hold the keys jointly with the Prophet, and after his loss by transgression, this authority was conferred on Hyrum Smith, then why do we not have today in the Church the same order of things, and an Assistant President as well as two counselors in the First Presidency?"

Then President Smith explained: "The answer to this is a simple one. It is because the peculiar condition requiring two witnesses to establish the work, is not required after the work is established. Joseph and Hyrum Smith stand at the head of this dispensation, jointly holding the keys, as the two necessary witnesses fulfilling the law as it is set down by our Lord in his answer to the Jews. Since the gospel will never again be restored there will be no occasion for this condition to arise again. We all look back to the two special witnesses, called to bear witness in full accord with the divine law." (Smith, *"The Divine Law of Witnesses—No Assistant* [Associate] *President Needed Today,"* ***Doctrines of Salvation***, Vol. 1, pp. 217–222).

22. The Prophet Joseph Smith, his brother Hyrum who served as Associate President of the Church, and Amasa Lyman who had been appointed to serve as a Counselor to the First Presidency, were the only members of the First Presidency the day of the Martyrdom. Sidney Rigdon had been set apart as First Counselor in the First Presidency on Monday, March 18, 1833, but had "not been in good standing for some

President of the Quorum of the Twelve at the time, and obedient to the procedures of Apostolic Succession, the Quorum of the Twelve had now to step forward and carry the burden of presidency over the whole Church with Brigham Young as their leader.

Brigham Young understood all of this—that "the keys of the kingdom are right here with the Church,"[23] others of the Quorum

---

years," and in the General Conference, Sunday, October 8, 1843, the Prophet had rejected him as a counselor. (Smith, ***History of the Church***, Vol. 6, pp. 48–49; ***Times and Seasons***, Vol. 5 [October 1, 1844], p. 663). Frederick G. Williams, the first Second Counselor in the First Presidency, was rejected Tuesday, November 7, 1837, and replaced by Hyrum Smith. (Smith, ***History of the Church***, Vol. 2, p. 522). Then when Hyrum Smith was ordained and set apart as Associate President on Sunday, January 24, 1841, William Law was appointed to succeed him (D&C 124:91, 97; Smith, ***History of the Church***, Vol. 4, 274–288), but William Law became disaffected and was excommunicated Thursday, April 18, 1844. (Smith, ***History of the Church***, Vol. 6, 341). Elder Orson Pratt, one of the first members of the Twelve, became disaffected briefly, and was excommunicated Saturday, August 20, 1842, but was baptized again Friday, January 20, 1843, and ordained and set apart again as a member of the Quorum of the Twelve. (Smith, ***History of the Church***, Vol. 5, pp. 255–256). Elder Amasa M. Lyman was appointed and ordained, Saturday, August 20, 1842, to fill the vacancy in the Quorum of the Twelve left by Elder Pratt's error. But shortly after Elder Pratt was reinstated, Elder Lyman visited the Prophet, who recorded, "I told him that I had restored Orson Pratt to the Quorum of the Twelve Apostles, and that I had concluded to make Brother Amasa Counselor in the First presidency," (Smith, ***History of the Church***, Vol. 5, p. 264). Thus, from the day of the Martyrdom, and continuing through the special meeting of Thursday, August 8, 1844, Amasa M. Lyman was the only man living, who had served with the First Presidency, who was yet faithful and in good standing in the Church. And although the death of the Prophet and his brother dissolved the First Presidency which Amasa Lyman had served as Counselor, he was an ordained Apostle, and was called and sustained as a member of the Quorum of the Twelve on Monday, August 12, 1844. (Smith, ***History of the Church***, Vol. 7

23. In a note about the Prophet's decision to surrender to Governor Thomas Ford and the mob masquerading as militia, Joseph Fielding Smith noted that "the Prophet did desire Hyrum Smith to succeed him in the presidency of the Church, and even 'ordained' him to take that place. At the October conference following the martyrdom of the two brothers, President Brigham Young said: 'Did Joseph ordain any man to

of the Twelve understood this,[24] and even a few of the Saints who had been privileged to be closely associated with the Prophet in Nauvoo understood this.[25] But many of the Saints were not

---

take his place? He did. Who was it? It was Hyrum. But Hyrum fell a martyr before Joseph did.'" (See Smith, ***History of the Church***, Vol. 6, p. 546; compare ***Times and Seasons***, October 15, 1844, Vol. 5, pp. 682–687).

The death of the President of the Church was without precedent in their experience, and they may be pardoned for wondering, in those moments when news of the Martyrdom was first confirmed to them, whether they had the authority to move forward. According to the record, when the martyrdom occurred, Brigham Young and others of the Twelve were serving missions in the East. In the first weeks of July, 1844, reports of travelers from Illinois and newspaper accounts began to appear claiming that the Prophet Joseph Smith and Hyrum Smith had been murdered. Even by the middle of July, Brigham Young and Orson Pratt, who were together in Petersboro, New Hampshire conducting a conference, had not believed the reports. But they received a letter from Wilford Woodruff, from Boston, dated Tuesday, July 16, 1844, reporting his receipt of letters from Erastus Snow and John E. Page which confirmed the death of Joseph and Hyrum "at Carthage." Brigham Young's first thought, as he later testified, was "whether Joseph had taken the keys of the kingdom with him from the earth." Brigham Young recalled that "Brother Orson Pratt sat on my left; we were leaning back in our chairs. Bringing my hand down on my knee I said, 'The keys of the kingdom are right here with the Church.'" Brigham Young and Orson Pratt then left Petersboro for Boston, staying over one night at Lowell, en route. On Thursday, July 18, from Boston, Brigham Young, with Wilford Woodruff acting as clerk, drafted an "Epistle of the Apostles to the Saints," which called for "all the authorities of the Church . . . such as the Presidents of the different Quorums, High Priests [and] Seventies" to assemble at Nauvoo "that we may meet them in Council as soon as convenient, as we expect to return immediately to Nauvoo." It was in these first days that Brigham Young's "great stout heart" broke, and he "gave vent to his feelings in tears." ("*Minutes*," ***Times and Seasons***, Vol. 5 [September 15, 1844], pp. 648–651; Smith, ***History of the Church***, Vol. 7, pp. 194–199, 284; President George Q. Cannon, "*Joseph's Legal Successor*," Tooele, Sunday afternoon, October 29, 1882, reported by George F. Gibbs, ***Deseret News Weekly***, Vol. 33 [February 21, 1883], pp. 66–67; ***Journal of Discourses***, 26 Volumes, Exact Lithographic Reprint of Original Edition [Salt Lake City, Utah: Deseret Book Company, 1978], Vol. 23, pp. 363–364).

24. Ibid., Monday, September 2, 1844, Vol. 5, pp. 637–638; Sunday, September 15, 1844. Vol. 5, pp. 647–655; Tuesday, October 1, 1844, Vol. 5, pp. 660–667; Tuesday, October 15, 1844, Vol. 5, pp. 682–687.

25. President George Q. Cannon, cited in Andrew Jenson, ***The Historical Record***,

aware of, or did not understand, the order of succession.[26] George Q. Cannon noted that members of the Twelve, as they hurried to return to Nauvoo, "had dreams and manifestations of the Spirit concerning" the matter. "But those at home were scarcely prepared . . . so unprepared, by any previous experience, for the steps that were necessary to carry on the work."[27]

And so, although he was immediately the Lord's mouthpiece on the earth by virtue of his senior position in the Quorum of the Twelve, Brigham Young still had to be sustained as the leader by a regularly constituted assembly of the

---

8 Vols. (Salt Lake City: The Andrew Jenson Publishing Company, 1887), Vol. 6, p. 791.

26. In the first General Conference that was convened after the death of President Brigham Young (October, 1877), only the second time in nearly fifty years that the Prophet and leader of the Church had been taken away, President George Q. Cannon taught:

> "Twice in our history, during the past forty-seven and a half years, have we been called to mourn the loss of him who has led the cause of the Holy Priesthood upon the earth. At both times the blow has fallen . . . unexpectedly . . . It was particularly so at the martyrdom of the Prophet Joseph Smith, for he had passed through so many difficulties, and had so many narrow escapes . . . that the Latter-day Saints had been led to regard him as almost invulnerable, and that his life would be spared to a good old age, if not to the winding up scene. His martyrdom, then, fell as [an] unexpected blow upon the people . . . ***a dreadful shock, for which a great bulk of the Latter-day Saints were unprepared.*** It is true that ***many were warned, especially those who were abroad among the nations preaching—they had dreams and manifestations of the Spirit*** concerning the terrible calamity. But those at home were scarcely prepared."

27. In the same address, October, 1877, President George Q. Cannon continued:

> "Evidences came so quickly, one after another, that there was scarcely an idea among the people that his arrest, or his delivering himself up as he did, would terminate in such a catastrophe. ***The Church itself was so unprepared, by any previous experience, for the steps that were necessary to carry on the work*** that the Lord had established, and of which he had been the instrument.
>
> "I well remember the feelings that were experienced upon that

Saints.[28] This assembly would be comprised of some members who knew, but also of others who "were at an entire loss to know who would take charge of the Church affairs."[29] Such an assembly was convened at Nauvoo in August, 1844.

---

occasion; how ***men's minds wondered, and the surmises that were indulged in; the guesses, the anticipations, some thinking one man would be chosen, and others that someone else would be. Many of the people were at an entire loss to know who would take charge of the Church affairs. And while they were not satisfied with Sidney Rigdon, nor his preaching, nor his propositions; a great many were undecided in their minds as to who would be the leader, or who would have the right to stand at the head.*** When the Twelve returned and their voices were heard in the midst of the people; when President Young stood before the congregation and spake to the people, doubt and uncertainty and every kindred feeling vanished, and every one who had a sufficient portion of the Spirit of the Lord recognized in him the man whom the Lord had chosen to lead and guide his people, instead of the martyred Prophet.

"For the first time in the history of the Church, the Twelve Apostles stepped forward and took the charge of affairs, by the authority of the Apostleship, and the authority which they had received from the Prophet Joseph. And for a little rising of three years they led and guided the Church, until the Lord inspired his servant Brigham, to organize a First Presidency of the Church. This experience has been most valuable to us under our present circumstances. Men have looked back to the past; they have remembered what was done at the period to which I refer, and doubt, uncertainty and hesitation have not existed to any extent; in fact, have not existed at all in the minds of those of long experience in the Church. The Twelve Apostles have the authority to lead and guide, to manage and direct the affairs of the Church, being the Quorum standing next to the First Presidency. Naturally it falls to them to step forward once more and assume the direction and control, to dictate and counsel and to regulate, so far as may be necessary, everything connected with the organization of the people, and the proclamation of the Gospel among the nations of the earth." (*"The Death of Joseph and the Death of Brigham,"* address at 47th Semi-annual General Conference, in the Tabernacle in Salt Lake City, Sunday morning, October 8, 1877, reported by George F. Gibbs, in ***Journal of Discourses***, Vol. 19, pp. 231–232, italics added).

28. D&C 26:2; 28:13; 38:34; 41:9; 102:9; 107:22.

29. Cannon, *"Revelation for the Guidance of the Church Comes Through the Head,"* in ***Journal of Discourses***, Vol. 19, pp. 231–232

The Saints Were As Sheep Without a Shepherd

At the time of the Martyrdom, most members of the Quorum of the Twelve were absent from the vicinity of Nauvoo by Joseph Smith's design.[30] Many of the Saints knew that the Twelve were in charge, but the Twelve were not fully assembled in Nauvoo—even by Thursday, August 1, 1844,

---

30. Of course, members of the Twelve were in Nauvoo in April, 1844, for the General Conference. At the General Conference, they planned a summer schedule of conferences to convene in the major cities, ending in Washington D. C. in September, with assignment of the Elders to fields of labor. Brigham Young closed the listing of assignments with the note: "the Twelve will devote the season to traveling, and will attend as many conferences as possible." The Prophet knew that the Twelve would be away from Nauvoo, and he expressed his desire that Hyrum leave as well. In late June, only two of the Twelve were in Nauvoo, Willard Richards, who acted as Nauvoo City Recorder, and John Taylor who was a City Councilor and Editor of the ***Times and Seasons***. When, by Thursday, June 20, 1844, matters in the vicinity of Nauvoo had deteriorated to where prospects of peaceful resolution appeared bleak, and knowing that soon his life would be taken, the Prophet "wrote to those of the Twelve Apostles who were absent on missions to come home immediately." In the period from Saturday, June 22 through Thursday, June 27, the Prophet and Hyrum foretold their deaths: Joseph, Saturday, June 22, just after dusk, in the upper room above Joseph's Nauvoo store: "there is no mercy—no mercy here." Hyrum, the same meeting: "just as sure as we fall into their hands we are dead men." Joseph, to Stephen Markham, outside the store after the meeting: "if I and Hyrum were ever taken again we should be massacred, or I was not a Prophet of God. I want Hyrum to live to lead the Church, but he is determined not to leave me." Joseph, Sunday, June 23, to Reynolds Cahoon, Lorenzo D. Wasson and Hiram Kimball, just after noon, in a house on the Iowa side of the river: "if my life is of no value to my friends it is of none to myself." Joseph, to Hyrum, just a few moments later: "I will go with you, but we shall be butchered." Joseph, Monday, June 24, to Hyrum, Henry G. Sherwood, Albert G. Fellows, Captain James E. Dunn of the Illinois State Militia, John Taylor, William W. Phelps, John P. Greene, Stephen C. Perry, Dimick B. Huntington, Jonathan Dunham, Stephen Markham, Jonathan Holmes, Jesse P. Harmon, John Lytle, Joseph W. Coolidge, David Harvey Redfield, Orrin P. Rockwell, Levi Richards, Willard Richards, Dan Jones, Alfred Randall, James Davis, Cyrus H. Wheelock, A. C. Hodge, James W. Woods and

only four[31] members of the Twelve had arrived at Nauvoo, and during this interim, while other members of the Twelve were gathering to Nauvoo as quickly as they were able, usurpers and traitors feigned commissions and authority, and even visions, to support their own improper claims to the right to

---

several others, at the Albert Fellows farm four miles west of Carthage: "I am going like a lamb to the slaughter, but I am calm as a summer's morning . . . I shall die an innocent man, and my blood shall cry from the ground for vengeance, and it shall be said of me, 'he was murdered in cold blood!'" (Smith, *"Difficulties,"* ***History of the Church***, Vol. 6, pp. 331–340, 486–487, 496, 519–520, 544–555).

Helen Mar Kimball Whitney recorded her opinion: "There seemed an overruling providence in the Apostles being away at the time of the martyrdom of Joseph and Hyrum, for the time had come for them to seal their testimony with their blood. If the Twelve had been there, they would never have permitted them to recross the river into Illinois, much less to be given up, as they were, quietly and without a struggle into the hands of a bloodthirsty mob," (*"Scenes and Incidents in Nauvoo,"* ***Woman's Exponent*** [Salt Lake City: The Church of Jesus Christ of Latter-day Saints] Vol. 11 [1882], p. 130. See footnote #114 below).

31. Willard Richards, ranked eighth in the Quorum, witnessed the martyrdom and arrived in Nauvoo the day after, Friday, June 28. John Taylor, ranked tenth in the Quorum, was wounded at Carthage and was brought to Nauvoo on Tuesday, July 2. Parley P. Pratt, ranked fourth in the Quorum at the time, had been laboring as a missionary in the East and returned to Nauvoo on Wednesday, July 10. "While Elder Pratt was en route from Chicago to Nauvoo, he learned by the whisperings of the Spirit that upon his arrival in Nauvoo, he should exert his influence to delay any action by the Church until the Quorum of the Twelve could be assembled. When he arrived in Nauvoo, he found that John Taylor and Willard Richards were of the same opinion and were urging the Saints to the same end." (Mouritsen, *"The Wolves Began to Prowl,"* ***The Office of Associate President***, p. 144; compare Parley P. Pratt, *"The Impressions of the Spirit at the Martyrdom of Joseph and Hyrum Smith,"* ***The Autobiography of Parley P. Pratt***, ed. Parley Parker Pratt, 4th Edition [Salt Lake City, Utah: Deseret Book Company, 1950], pp. 333–334). Mary Ann Winters recalled that "Brother [Parley P.] Pratt . . . brought the sunlight of the Holy Spirit with him—faith, hope, courage and strength—cheer to press onward undaunted. The burden seemed lifted, for he came with the power of the Holy Priesthood, and the light of revelation . . . and the hearts of the faithful turned from their sorrow to the up-holding and sustaining of the work that our beloved Prophet and Patriarch had laid down their lives as a sacrifice for. Each day . . . he brought us fresh words of encouragement, and soon Brother Brigham,

lead.[32] Brigham Young testified that, upon his return to Nauvoo, it was apparent that "many wanted to draw off a party and be leaders."[33] Wilford Woodruff, one of the Quorum of the Twelve who arrived in Nauvoo the evening of Tuesday, August 6, 1844, recalled that "a deep gloom seemed to rest over the city of Nauvoo, which we never experienced before." He recorded that the next morning, August 7,

> *"I went forth . . . through the city of Nauvoo, saw many friends, and met with the Quorum of the Twelve at Elder Taylor's. We were truly glad to see each other. Brother Taylor was getting well of his wounds that he received in Jail in company with Joseph and Hyrum Smith when they were murdered. We were glad to see Dr. Richards, who escaped unhurt. We were received with gladness by the Saints throughout the city; they felt like sheep without a shepherd, as being without a father, as their head had been taken away."*[34]

Brother Kimball and the others arrived, each filled with the spirit of their calling . . . and though the gloom could be plainly felt, the rod of iron was there, and the majority took strong hold and walked firmly on even unto the end of their days on earth." ("*The Autobiography of Mary Ann Sterns Winters, 1833–1853*," Typescript, Historical Department, The Church of Jesus Christ of Latter-day Saints [hereafter Church Historical Department], Salt Lake City, pp. 24–25). George A. Smith, ranked eleventh in the Quorum, had been laboring as a missionary in Michigan and arrived at Nauvoo on Sunday, July 28. (***The Historical Record***, Vol. 6, pp. 780–785).

32. There were a number of others, but the challenge of Sidney Rigdon was, in this judgment, the most formidable. See Dr. Russell R. Rich, "*Preface*," ***Those Who Would Be Leaders: Offshoots of Mormonism***, 2nd ed. (Provo: Brigham Young University Press, 1967), pp. 1–3.

33. Diary of Brigham Young (Manuscript History of Brigham Young), Church Historical Department, Thursday, August 8, 1844; hereafter, Diary of Brigham Young.

34. Journal of Wilford Woodruff, Wilford Woodruff Collection, Church Historical Department, Salt Lake City, August 6–7, 1844; hereafter Journal of Wilford Woodruff.

Brigham Young observed of the Saints that they "looked as though they had lost a friend [Joseph Smith] that was able and willing to counsel them in all things."[35]

Sidney Rigdon Wanted to Act Before the Twelve Returned

Word had spread throughout Nauvoo that Sidney Rigdon had arrived on Saturday, August 3, 1844. Perhaps because of his age or previous eloquence, or out of deference to his former station, Sidney Rigdon enjoyed a measure of respect among the Saints. The following morning, at 10:00 AM, a substantial congregation of Latter-day Saints assembled for the traditional Sabbath worship services at the Stand, in the "grove" as they called it, just east of the Temple site.

Normally the Saints conducted both a morning and an afternoon meeting on the Sabbath day, and in the morning meeting, Sidney Rigdon preached a discourse.[36] He told the assembled Saints of a supposed revelation which he had received directing him that a guardian must now be appointed

---

35. Diary of Brigham Young, Thursday, August 8, 1844.

36. Sidney Rigdon had served as First Counselor in the First Presidency, but the Prophet had "rejected" or released him—despite the overruling "vote" of the Saints, at the Semi-annual General Conference, Sunday, October 8, 1843, at Nauvoo. The Prophet's death dissolved the First Presidency, and since Sidney Rigdon had never been ordained an Apostle or designated a member of the Twelve, and therefore had no standing in that body, he was no longer an authority of the Church. In light of this, and because Sidney Rigdon had not been valiant in his calling for some years, had left Nauvoo and taken his family to Pittsburgh in defiance of the Lord's specific instruction to him, and was even thought by some to have encouraged enemies of the Church, the graciousness of the Twelve toward him, and their patience and kindness to him during this period, must be regarded as extraordinary. (D&C 124:103–110; "*Continuation,*" ***Times and Seasons***, Vol. 5 [October 1, 1844], pp. 660–669).

to lead the Church and conduct its affairs.[37] The balance of his remarks consisted in a rather lengthy "harangue" to the Saints about his own qualifications for the post.

In the afternoon gathering on that same Sabbath day, at Sidney Rigdon's request, a call was issued for the Saints to assemble on Thursday, August 8, at 10:00 AM, to appoint a guardian for the Church.[38] At the time of these Sunday meetings, only a few of the Twelve Apostles were, as yet, present in Nauvoo—Parley P. Pratt, John Taylor, George A. Smith and Willard Richards, and they vigorously and courageously, in the uncertainties of those threatening days, opposed "this hasty step."[39] The former counselor to Joseph Smith had continually reassured them that he would not proceed to request the Saints to take any official action until others of the Quorum of the Twelve could assemble, but by his actions at these Sunday meetings, his purposes were exposed and it became clear that

37. When he arrived at Nauvoo, Tuesday evening, August 6, 1844, and learned of Sidney Rigdon's claimed manifestation setting forth the specious arrangement in which Sidney was to act as the "spokesman" for the Prophet Joseph Smith, Wilford Woodruff contemptuously referred to it as a "kind of second class vision." Journal of Wilford Woodruff, Wednesday, August 7, 1844.

38. During the "afternoon: Elders Murdock and Rich preached. Elder William Marks, President of the [Nauvoo] Stake, gave public notice (at the request of Elder Rigdon), that there would be a special meeting of the Church at the Stand, on Thursday, the 8th inst., for the purpose of choosing a guardian, (President and Trustee). Elder Thomas Grover proposed waiting . . . Elder Marks said President Rigdon wanted the meeting on Tuesday, but he put it off till Thursday; that Elder Rigdon was some distance from his family, and wanted to know if this people had anything for him to do; if not, he wanted to go on his way, for there was a people numbering thousands and tens of thousands who would receive him; that he wanted to visit other branches around, but he had come here first." (Smith, *"The Gathering of the Twelve Apostles From the East To Nauvoo: Preliminary Meetings Looking To the Settlement of the Question of the Presidency of the Church," **History of the Church***, Vol. 7, p. 225).

39. Helen Mar Kimball Whitney recorded that "a day was appointed by [William]

his intent was to try to electioneer himself into a position of leadership before the absent members of the Apostleship could return. "The fact was he hoped to carry out his design before they could reach the city of Nauvoo," George Q. Cannon noted. "It was no part of his scheme to wait for them."[40]

Other men present in Nauvoo that Sunday—loyal to the Quorum of the Twelve, (among them, Charles C. Rich, William Clayton and Thomas Grover), made every effort to postpone the designation of any meeting to choose a new leader for the

---

Marks, the president of the stake, for a special conference to choose a guardian. Brothers Willard Richards, Parley P. Pratt, John Taylor and George A. Smith were opposed to this hasty step, and the former counseled the Saints not to be in a hurry, but to wait until the Twelve Apostles returned." ("*Scenes and Incidents in Nauvoo*," ***Women's Exponent***, Vol. 11 [1882], p. 130. See footnote #114 below).

40. President George Q. Cannon, cited in Andrew Jenson, ***The Historical Record***, Vol. 7, p. 781. During the interval from the day of the Martyrdom "until the arrival of President Brigham Young and the Twelve, Elder Willard Richards was the principal counselor of the Saints in Nauvoo and had scarcely a moment to rest. He answered the calls and inquiries of hundreds of the brethren, and was engaged every day until a late hour, or until exhaustion compelled him to lie down." (Smith, ***History of the Church***, Vol. 7, pp. 183, 184, 200, 222, 228). Elder Parley P. Pratt arrived July 10, 1844, and as the ranking member of the Twelve in Nauvoo at the time, consulted regularly with Willard Richards, John Taylor and George A. Smith. He also defended the Twelve, and sought to delay any action by others until the Twelve could return to Nauvoo. (Smith, ***History of the Church***, Vol. 7, pp. 176, 184, 190, 200, 202, 212, 222–228). The courage demonstrated by Willard Richards and John Taylor, the two members of the Twelve in Nauvoo immediately after the Martyrdom, Parley P. Pratt and George A. Smith who joined them in July, and the other brethren who sought to delay any action by Sidney Rigdon or by the Church until the members of the Twelve were finally able to assemble in Nauvoo in early August, is remarkable. Certainly their lives were in danger. On Sunday, June 30, 1844, Willard Richards wrote to Brigham Young at Boston: "You now know our situation, and the request of the council is, that the Twelve return to Nauvoo. The ***lives of twelve more*** [the Twelve] ***are threatened with deadly threats***. It has been suggested by the council, that if the Twelve approved, President Brigham Young, Heber C. Kimball, George A. Smith, Wilford Woodruff and Orson Pratt return immediately; and William Smith, whose life is threatened, with all the Smiths, John E. Page, Lyman

Church until the other Apostles could be present to participate, but their objections were sounded to no avail, and plans for the Thursday meeting apparently proceeded.[41]

Brigham Young and Others of the Twelve Reached Nauvoo

Brigham Young and others of the Quorum were landed at "the upper stone house" at Nauvoo by the river steamer St. Croix at 8:00 PM on Tuesday evening, August 6.[42] The next morning, Brigham Young assembled members of the Twelve—perhaps as many as ten of them—Heber C. Kimball, probably Orson Hyde, Parley P. Pratt, Orson Pratt, Willard Richards, Wilford Woodruff, George A. Smith and possibly Lyman Wight, for a council meeting at the home of John Taylor who was still

---

Wight, Parley P. Pratt and Orson Hyde spend a little time in publishing the news in the eastern cities, and getting as many in the Church as possible. This is for you to decide." (Smith, ***History of the Church***, Vol. 7, p. 147, italics and brackets added). President Brigham Young, in the meeting at Seventies' Hall, declared: "I know there are those in our midst who will seek the lives of the Twelve as they did the lives of Joseph and Hyrum," (Smith, ***History of the Church***, Vol. 7, p. 230). And on Thursday, August 8, President Young stated: "I do not know whether my enemies will take my life or not, and I do not care, for I want to be with the man I love," (Smith, ***History of the Church***, Vol. 7, p. 233). We know there were parties bent on destruction of the Prophet and the Church prior to the Martyrdom. The history includes reports of activities of enemies of the Church following the Martyrdom. These were directed primarily against Brigham Young, others of the Twelve, and those loyal to the Twelve. These reports provide ample testimony that all these brethren had reason to feel their activities to press forward with the organization of the Church, construction on the Temple, and to seek redress for the atrocities committed against the Saints, would further provoke the enemies of the Church, and that their lives were in danger. They proceeded anyway for they were the servants of God and they knew it. (See Smith, ***History of the Church***, Vol. 6, pp. 463, 482, 497, 502; Vol. 7, pp. 130, 254, 353, 403–423, 442, 490).

41. Jenson, ***The Historical Record***, Vol. 7, pp. 785–786.

42. Smith, ***History of the Church***, Vol. 7, p. 228.

convalescing from his wounds received at Carthage.[43] At that meeting, it was decided that members of the Twelve, the High Council, and the High Priests should convene later that same day in a council at the nearly completed Seventies Hall.

When that meeting got underway at 4:00 PM in the afternoon of August 7, Sidney Rigdon, who was present, was invited by Brigham Young to make a statement to the assembly to explain his presence and purposes in Nauvoo.[44] In response to this opportunity, the man that the Prophet Joseph Smith had rejected as a counselor announced that he had come to Nauvoo to magnify the appointment that he had received to act as "spokesman" for the Prophet: "I have been ordained as the spokesman to Joseph, and I must come to Nauvoo and see that the Church is governed in a proper manner."[45]

---

43. This made a total of probably ten members of the Twelve who attended the meeting at the home of John Taylor. It may be that as many as three members of the Twelve were as yet absent from Nauvoo: perhaps Orson Hyde, ranked third in the Quorum, who traveled with Brigham Young and the others from New York toward Nauvoo, but who left them at Fairport, Ohio, to visit his family in Kirtland. He certainly had arrived at Nauvoo by Thursday, August 8, because he later spoke of being present at the momentous meetings of that day, and on Sunday, August 25, for he preached that day at the Stand, (Smith, ***History of the Church***, Vol. 7, p. 211); William Smith, ranked fifth in the Quorum, and who, obedient to the wisdom of the Twelve, remained in the East and presided over a conference in Philadelphia on Sunday, September 1, 1844, (Smith, ***History of the Church***, Vol. 7, p. 266); and John E. Page, ranked seventh in the Quorum, who, obedient to the wisdom of the Twelve, remained at Pittsburgh and did not return to Nauvoo until the dedication of the Seventies' Hall, Thursday, December 26, 1844, (Smith, ***History of the Church***, Vol. 7, pp. 330–343). It is not clear when Elder Hyde returned to Nauvoo, but from his own record he arrived in time to be present at the meeting at the Stand on Thursday, August 8, 1844, (see footnote #71 below).

44. Jenson, ***The Historical Record***, Vol. 7, p. 788.

45. Smith, "*Meeting of Twelve Apostles, High Council and High Priests at Seventies' Hall,*" ***History of the Church***, Vol. 7, p. 229. Compare Prophet Joseph Smith, "*How and By Whom Revelation Comes,*" ***Teachings of the Prophet Joseph Smith***, Compiled by

Sidney Rigdon Presented His Claims to the Brethren

Then Sidney Rigdon attempted to establish his claims to position and leadership. Certainly unclear, strange and variant from the channels of revelation the Prophet Joseph Smith had described, Sidney Rigdon appeared to suggest that the Prophet Joseph, from his vantage point in the eternal worlds, "sustains the same relationship to this Church as he has always done," and that "there must be revelation still." Then, the former counselor to the Prophet asserted, since "the martyred Prophet is still the head of this Church" and "I [Sidney Rigdon] was commanded to speak for him," the mourning Saints had no other alternative but to acknowledge that revelations from Joseph Smith would have to come through Sidney Rigdon to the Church.

Joseph Fielding Smith, 19th Printing, 2nd Printing of Edition with an Index prepared by Robert J. Matthews (Salt Lake City: Deseret Book Company, 1985), p. 111.

Benjamin Ashby recalled that "Brother Willard Richards was the only one of the Twelve Apostles who was in Nauvoo. John Taylor, being wounded, remained in Carthage. Soon the Twelve began to return." (Benjamin Ashby, "*Autobiography*," holograph, L. Tom Perry Special Collections, Harold B. Lee Library, Brigham Young University, pp. 10–11).

Benjamin Ashby was born in Salem, Massachusetts in 1828. the son of a shoemaker. He heard the Gospel preached by Elder Erastus Snow in 1840, and was baptized with his father's family in 1842. They relocated to Nauvoo in December, 1843. He was sixteen years old when he attended the meeting at the Stand, Thursday, August 8, 1844. He worked with George Q. Cannon, who was just a year older than he was, digging a trench for a wall around the Nauvoo Temple—the wall was not completed. He received his blessings in the Nauvoo Temple, buried his father on the trek west, aided his mother with the care of his ten siblings, later served a mission to England, married Ann Chester—they had eleven sons and three daughters, served as a Patriarch, and labored in the Salt Lake Temple from 1893 until his death at Bountiful, Davis County, Utah, on Tuesday, November 19, 1907, at the age of 79.

In this appeal, Sidney Rigdon did not claim to take the Prophet's place, nor did he lay any specious claims to authority. He simply declared that since he had once "been consecrated a spokesman to Joseph," the Church would have to put up with him as the conduit of information from that heaven where Joseph had gone.[46] He even went so far as to suggest that a solemn assembly should be held, that the Church should stand together in priesthood quorums "as you

---

46. Smith, ***History of the Church***, Vol. 7, p. 229. In 1833, the Lord had called Sidney Rigdon to "be a spokesman unto this people; yea, verily, I will ordain you unto this calling, even to be a spokesman unto my servant Joseph . . . And I will give unto thee power to be mighty in expounding all scriptures, that thou mayest be a spokesman unto him, and he shall be a revelator unto thee, that thou mayest know the certainty of all things pertaining to . . . my kingdom . . ." (D&C 100:9, 11). Then eight years later, the Lord revealed:

> ". . . if my servant Sidney will . . . be counselor unto my servant Joseph, let him arise and come up and stand in the office of his calling, and humble himself before me.
>
> "And if he will offer unto me an acceptable offering, and acknowledgments, and remain with my people, behold, I, the Lord your God, will heal him . . . and he shall lift up his voice again on the mountains, and be a spokesman before my face . . .
>
> "Let him come and locate his family in the neighborhood in which my servant Joseph resides.
>
> "Let him assist my servant Joseph . . .
>
> "If my servant Sidney will do my will, let him not remove his family unto the eastern lands . . .
>
> "Behold, ***it is not my will that he shall seek to find safety and refuge out of the city which I have appointed unto you, even the city of Nauvoo***.
>
> "Verily I say unto you, even now, if he will hearken unto my voice, it shall be well with him. Even so. Amen." (D&C 124:103–110).

At a special conference on Friday, October 6, 1843, at Nauvoo, the Prophet rejected Sidney Rigdon as a Counselor in the First Presidency, (Smith, ***History of the Church***, Vol. 6, p. 47. See footnote #50 below, for an account of Sidney Rigdon's rejection). Subsequently, Sidney Rigdon attended the General Conference of the Church in April, 1844, at Nauvoo, and is mentioned frequently in Church activities in Nauvoo until after the April Conference. But despite "all his fair promises of amendment,

stood in your washings and consecrations" for the apparent design that they sustain him in the position he claimed.[47]

The President of the Quorum of Twelve Apostles was the next to speak, and he reminded those present that the "means of obtaining the mind of God on the subject" were with him because he was the first among that body of men upon which the Prophet had conferred "all the keys and powers belonging to the Apostleship which he himself held before he was taken away." Brigham Young then called upon the brethren present to sustain a resolution that members of the Church and members of the various priesthood quorums assemble in their proper order in a meeting to convene the following week, on Tuesday, August 13, 1844. His resolution carried unanimously.[48]

Sidney Rigdon continued neglectful of his high duties . . . He longed to return to the east, and notwithstanding the Lord had commanded him to make his home at Nauvoo, he frequently talked with President Smith about going to Pittsburgh to live, and finally obtained his consent to go there, and take his family with him. He was instructed to preach, write, and build up the church in that city." (B. H. Roberts, ***Comprehensive History of the Church***, 6 Volumes, Exact Lithographic Reprint of 1930 Edition [Provo, Utah: Brigham Young University Press, 1965], Vol. 2, p. 423). Upon learning of the death of the Prophet, Sidney Rigdon returned to Nauvoo, arriving Saturday, August 3, 1844, whereupon he commenced his campaign to assume the leadership of the Church, (Smith, ***History of the Church***, Vol. 7, p. 222).

47. Jenson, ***The Historical Record***, Vol. 7, p. 789.

48. Smith, ***History of the Church***, Vol. 7, p. 230. B. H. Roberts evidently believed that Brigham Young actually called this meeting to convene at 10:00 AM on Thursday, August 8; however, the Journal of Wilford Woodruff, August 8, 1844; ***The Millennial Star***, 25:216; the Journal History of The Church of Jesus Christ of Latter-day Saints, August 7, 1844, Historical Department, Salt Lake City, and many private diaries and journals all state that Brigham Young, apparently in council with his brethren of the Twelve, did call the meeting in question to convene Tuesday, August 13, 10:00 AM. President Brigham Young's restraint in this challenging period is noteworthy. He had every right to act quickly, but instead, appears to have determined to study the situation and the attitude of Sidney Rigdon, and to assess the feelings of the Saints, before proceeding.

The Saints Gathered at the Stand

On Thursday morning, August 8, 1844, at 10:00, the Saints gathered at the Stand for the "prayer meeting" that had been proposed by Sidney Rigdon and called by William Marks.[49] This was to be a different meeting than the important assembly appointed by the Twelve to convene the following Tuesday, August 13. Still, the anxiety apparent among the Saints, and concerns harbored by some of the leading brethren about the true intentions of Sidney Rigdon, were sufficient that Brigham Young and others of the Twelve appear to have felt that they should be present at Thursday's "prayer meeting" or at least join the meeting in course.

Sidney Rigdon was perhaps the most conspicuous figure at the assembly. The Saints had sustained him as First Counselor in the First Presidency only months before, although the Prophet had rejected him.[50] And many of the Saints knew that he had left Nauvoo and moved to Pittsburgh, Pennsylvania following the April 1844 General Conference, and that he had

---

49. Jenson, ***The Historical Record,*** Vol 7, p. 789.

50. The minutes of a special conference called to investigate President Sidney Rigdon's standing as a Counselor in the First Presidency conclude that "on motion by President William Marks, and seconded by Patriarch Hyrum Smith, [the] conference voted that Elder Sidney Rigdon be permitted to retain his station as Counselor in the First Presidency. President Joseph Smith arose and said, 'I have thrown him off my shoulders, and you have again put him on me. You may carry him, but I will not,'" (Smith, ***History of the Church,*** Vol. 6, pp. 47–49). This is corroborated by many private journals and diaries.

A constituent assembly of Latter-day Saints may sustain a call, and offer a vote of thanks for service rendered upon a release, but the assembly cannot extend a call or a release. The assembly, or individual members of the assembly, may raise an objection to a call if they feel they have knowledge of unworthiness, unknown to the presiding officers, that would disqualify the person called from serving. But there is no reason

returned to Nauvoo from Pittsburgh about a month after the Prophet's death, arriving only days before.

Sidney Rigdon, William Marks—who at the time served as the President of the Nauvoo Stake, and others including some of the Twelve, but apparently not Brigham Young, occupied seats on the Stand, at the traditional meeting ground located just east of the Temple site. But because the wind was blowing from a direction behind the congregation and toward the Stand, and in an effort to make himself heard, Sidney Rigdon, accompanied by William Marks, got down from the Stand, moved to the back, and climbed into a wagon "which was

---

that the assembly or individual members of the assembly could be justified in raising an objection to a release. President Joseph Fielding Smith explained:

> "No man can preside in this Church in any capacity without the consent of the people. The Lord has placed upon us the responsibility of sustaining by vote those who are called to various positions of responsibility. No man, should the people decide to the contrary, could preside over any body of Latter-day Saints in this Church, and yet it ***is not the right of the people to nominate, to choose, for that is the right of the priesthood.***
>
> ***"The priesthood selects,*** under the inspiration of our Father in heaven, and then it is the duty of the Latter-day Saints, as they are assembled in conference, or other capacity, by the uplifted hand, to sustain or to reject; and I take it that no man has the right to raise his hand in opposition, or with contrary vote, unless he has a reason for doing so that would be valid if presented before those who stand at the head . . . I have no right to raise my hand in opposition to a man who is appointed to any position in this Church, simply because I may not like him, or because of some personal disagreement or feeling I may have, but only on the grounds that he is guilty of wrong doing, of transgression of the laws of the Church which would disqualify him for the position which he is called to hold." (Smith, *"Operation of the Law of Common Consent within the Church,"* ***Doctrines of Salvation,*** Vol. 3, p. 123, italics added. Compare President John Taylor, *"The Martyrdom,"* ***The Gospel Kingdom,*** Edited by G. Homer Durham, 2nd printing of Collector's Edition [Salt Lake City: Bookcraft, 1990], pp. 358–364).

Therefore, a constituent assembly may raise objections to a call, subject to defined limations, but a constituent assembly has absolutely no authority to raise objections to

drawn up" behind the congregation, with the thought that the wind would carry his words out across the congregation and toward the Stand. Accordingly, all of the Saints present (Brigham Young, who arrived later, estimated the assembly to be about five thousand in number[51]) turned themselves about to face the wagon, at the rear of the assembly, into which the apparently weary and listless Sidney Rigdon had climbed.[52]

Sidney Rigdon Addressed the Saints

Perhaps by design, but probably because he was engaged in discussions with the Twelve throughout most of that unsettled August morning, Brigham Young arrived after the meeting had begun, but with their backs to the Stand, the Saints did not notice him as he made his way up onto the Stand to occupy the seat that Sidney Rigdon had vacated in his decision to remove to the wagon.[53] So there they were, about five thousand members of the Church, with their leaders upon

---

a release. The man who held all of the keys and authority to release Sidney Rigdon as First Counselor in the First Presidency had in fact released him. Sidney Rigdon was therefore released.

51. Diary of Brigham Young, August 8, 1844.

52. On another occasion, George Q. Cannon testified that "after the martyrdom of the Prophet the Twelve soon returned to Nauvoo, and learned of the aspirations of Sidney Rigdon. He had claimed that the Church needed a guardian, and that he was that guardian. He had appointed the day for the guardian to be selected, and of course was present at the meeting, which was held in the open air. ***The wind was blowing toward the Stand so strongly at the time that an improvised stand was made out of a wagon, which was drawn up at the back part of the congregation, and which he, William Marks, and some others occupied.*** He attempted to speak, but was much embarrassed. He had been the orator of the Church; but, on this occasion his oratory failed him, and his talk fell very flat. In the meantime President Young and some of his brethren came and entered the Stand." (*"Joseph's Legal Successor,"* ***Journal of Discourses***, Vol. 23, pp.363–364).

53. George Q. Cannon, ***The Juvenile Instructor***, October 29, 1870, Vol. 5, pp. 174–5,

the Stand behind them, all facing into the wind to hear what Sidney Rigdon might have to say.

"Usually Sidney Rigdon was a fluent, impassioned speaker, and excelled in oratory," George Q. Cannon noted, "but upon this occasion he was visibly embarrassed, and spoke slowly and in a very labored manner." And further, "this meeting" comprised "a grand gathering of earnest, sorrowful men and women. Their earthly head had been taken away from them . . . the Prophet of God was slain, and there was anxiety to know who should act in his stead and lead them as he had done."[54]

Instead of speaking directly to the question pressing upon the minds of many in the anxious assembly, Sidney Rigdon "talked much" about "the Mount of Olives, the Brook Kedron, Queen Victoria, great battles, but said little about Nauvoo or the Prophet Joseph. He had, in fact, lost all contact with the people, with facts, and above all, with the flame and torch of divine authority. Even his few friends

---

182. What an extraordinary scene! Winds of sufficient strength that Sidney Rigdon moved from the Stand to a wagon! And what kept Brigham Young that he came later to the Stand? Certainly the Lord whose Church it is, who "knoweth all things, and there is not anything save he knows it" (2 Nephi 9:20), and who has "all power, both in heaven and in earth" (Mosiah 4:9), even the power to control the wind (Jonah 1:4; Psalms 104:3; Mark 4:41), had an interest in the proceedings of that assembly. And He can, and He does, orchestrate all that may be necessary to bring about His divine and holy purposes. (Compare 1 Nephi 1:20; D&C 33:5–13; 65:2–3).

54. Cannon, ***The Juvenile Instructor***, October 29, 1870, Vol. 5, pp. 174–175, 182. At another time, President Cannon explained: "It was necessary that there should be some manifestation of the power of God, because the people were divided. There was considerable of doubt as to who should lead the Church. People had supposed that Joseph would live to redeem Zion. They felt very much as the disciples did after the crucifixion: 'We trusted,' said they to the Savior, whom they knew not, while speaking of their Lord, 'that it had been He which should have redeemed Israel' [Luke 24:21].

were disillusioned."[55] His words, as George Q. Cannon later wrote, "awakened no emotions; they touched no heart; they were destitute of the Spirit, and they, therefore, had no effect upon the people, except to strengthen the conviction that he was not the man chosen by the Almighty to be their leader."[56] "They heard from him no voice or sound that marked him as the true shepherd."[57]

Decision to Reassemble the Saints that Afternoon

As Brigham Young looked down from his chair on the Stand, and out across the assembled Saints seated or standing with their backs to him as they listened to the address of Sidney Rigdon, he noted their sadness and dejection. Only six weeks had passed since the Martyrdom. But instead of hearing words of comfort and reassurance, or declarations of unity among the leading Brethren, the Saints were obliged to listen to Sidney Rigdon present a labored, hollow-sounding, claim to be the "guardian" of the Church. Now *prophets* was a term they understood. And the term *apostles* was familiar to them. But what was a guardian? The Prophet Joseph Smith had never spoken to them about a "guardian." The revelations contained no mention of the term. Brigham Young recorded that "in this

---

They were saddened in their hearts. So the Saints were when the Prophet Joseph was taken from them. Some even went so far as to think that perhaps God would resurrect him, they had such an idea about his continued earthly connection with this work." (*"Joseph Smith the Head of this Dispensation—The Twelve Ordained by Him to Bear off the Kingdom—Joseph's Legal Successor,"* ***Journal of Discourses***, Vol. 23, pp. 363–364).

55. Susa Young Gates and Leah D. Widtsoe, ***The Life Story of Brigham Young*** (New York City: The MacMillan Company, 1930), p. 40.

56. Cannon, ***The Juvenile Instructor***, October 29, 1870, Vol. 5, pp. 174–5, 182.

57. Cannon, in Jenson, ***The Historical Record***, Vol. 7, p. 789.

time of sorrow, my heart was filled with compassion" toward them.[58]

It is not clear when the decision was reached to change the day of the meeting originally scheduled for the following Tuesday, August 13, to that very afternoon, Thursday, August 8. The decision was obviously made after the meeting at Seventies' Hall the preceding afternoon, and was perhaps made by Brigham Young there at the Stand as he listened to Sidney Rigdon present his claims of precedence to the Saints. Wilford Woodruff left the impression that Brigham Young made the decision "at the office" in conversation with his brethren of the Twelve who were able to meet, for he wrote,

> *". . . in consequence of some excitement among the people and a disposition by some spirit to try to divide the Church, it was thought best to attend to the business of the Church in the afternoon that was to be attended to on [the following] Tuesday. The Twelve spent their time in the forepart of the day at the office and in the afternoon, met at the grove."*[59]

Sidney Rigdon continued with his address for about an hour and a half, "without interruption," and sat down at approximately 11:30 AM.[60] "The wind by this time had ceased to blow."[61] It was at that moment that Brigham Young arose from his position on the Stand and began to speak.

---

58. Diary of Brigham Young, August 8, 1844.

59. Journal of Wilford Woodruff, August 8, 1844.

60. B. H. Roberts, *"Confusion—Choosing a Leader,"* ***The Rise and Fall of Nauvoo*** (Salt Lake City: Deseret News Press, 1960), pp. 328–329.

61. Cannon, *"Joseph's Legal Successor,"* ***Journal of Discourses***, Vol. 23, pp. 363–364.

Sidney Rigdon Ended His Speech from the Wagon and Brigham Young Arose on the Stand

During the course of Sidney Rigdon's long address that morning, Benjamin F. Johnson[62] was seated between the Stand and the wagon occupied by Sidney Rigdon. Just at the moment that Sidney Rigdon concluded his address, Benjamin Johnson turned to face the Stand, perhaps assuming that any further discussion in that assembly would come from the Stand. He saw Brigham Young stand up,

> *". . . but as soon as he spoke I jumped upon my feet, for in every possible degree it was Joseph's voice, and his person,*

62. Benjamin F. Johnson was born Tuesday, July 28, 1818, in Pomfret, Chatauqua County, New York, the fifth son and tenth child in a family of sixteen. His mother and siblings were among the first to embrace the Restoration. He was not of age then, but in 1835, over the objections of his father, he was baptized by Elder Lyman Johnson, one of the first Apostles, and received his patriarchal blessing under the hand of Joseph Smith, Senior. His acquaintance with the Prophet Joseph began in Kirtland, and in the next decade, he became one of the Prophet's trusted, intimate friends. He lived his life in parallel with the growth and movement of the Church from Ohio to Missouri to Illinois to Utah. During the Missouri persecutions in 1838, when just 20 years old, Benjamin was directed to denounce the Prophet or he would be shot; he refused. Twice his assailant aimed and pulled the trigger, but the gun misfired. The third time, the gun exploded, killing the attacker. He was in Nauvoo on Thursday, August 8, 1844, and witnessed the events which are the subject of this study. He managed the Mansion house until the Saints left Nauvoo. In Utah he settled Santaquin in 1851, served a mission in the Hawaiian Islands, returned in 1853 to assist with the construction of a fort and to resettle Santaquin, later serving as Bishop in Spring Lake, and then as Patriarch. In his last years, he moved to Mesa, Arizona, where, two years prior to his death and in response to a request from George F. Gibbs, Secretary to the First Presidency, he wrote an extended letter of his recollections of the Prophet Joseph Smith. On Saturday, November 18, 1905, he died, at the age of 87 years. (See ***My Life's Review***; and *"Benjamin F. Johnson to George F. Gibbs, 1903,"* LDS Church Archives. See also E. Dale LeBaron, ***Benjamin Franklin Johnson: Colonizer, Public Servant, and Church Leader,***

> *in look, attitude, dress and appearance, [it] was Joseph himself, personified; and I knew in a moment the spirit and mantle of Joseph was upon him. Then I remembered [the Prophet's] saying to the Council [of the Twelve] of which Sidney Rigdon was never a member, and I knew for myself who was now the leader of Israel. New confidence and joy continued to spring up within me . . ."*[63]

"Although only a boy, I saw the mantle of the Prophet Joseph rest on Brigham Young," recalled Mosiah Lyman Hancock. "I saw Brother Brigham Young, of the Quorum of the Twelve, arise before the people—and I saw in him the look of Joseph, and the voice of Joseph; and it seemed to me that he

---

[Master's thesis, 1967], L. Tom Perry Special Collections, Harold B. Lee Library, Brigham Young University, Provo, Utah], pp. 325–46).

63. Benjamin F. Johnson, ***My Life's Review*** (Independence, Missouri: Zion's Printing and Publishing Company, 1928), pp. 103–104. On another occasion, Benjamin Johnson testified that "this view, or vision, although but for seconds, was to me as vivid and real as the glare of lightning or the voice of thunder from the heavens, and so deeply was I impressed with what I saw and heard in this transfiguration, that for years I dare not publicly tell what was given me of the Lord to see. But when in later years I did publicly bear this testimony, I found that others would testify to having seen and heard the same. But to what proportion of the congregation who were present I could never know. But I do know that this, my testimony, is true." (***My Life's Review***, p. 343).

The Prophet's "saying," to which Benjamin F. Johnson alludes, was perhaps his statement to the Twelve, as they assembled in meetings in the room above the Prophet's store in Nauvoo, in April, 1844, to which Benjamin F. Johnson, Bathsheba W. Smith, and a number of other trusted Saints were invited, as recalled by Wilford Woodruff in a general letter to the Saints: "I will commence by asking where has Elder Rigdon been . . . Has he stood by the side of the Prophet and Patriarch as a true friend, to assist in carrying them through their trials, tribulations and persecutions? Has he walked up into his place as a man of God, and stood beside the Prophet as his counselor . . . Has he sustained the cause and used an influence to spread the work abroad since the persecution in Far West? Has he in any way sustained the priesthood with

was as tall as Joseph too. I knew that the mantle of Joseph had fallen on Brigham." Then he wrote, "I had heard the Prophet say from the frame [the Stand] that he threw the furtherance of this Church and Kingdom upon the shoulders of the Twelve[64] [and] that they should . . . send this Gospel to every nation under heaven." "Brigham Young," he concluded,

---

dignity and honor, for the last five years of his life? Or, has the Prophet, in any point of view, leaned upon him as a counselor, a staff, or support, for the last five years? Or has the Prophet Joseph found Elder Rigdon in his councils when he organized the quorum of the Twelve, a few months before his death, to prepare them for the endowment? And when they received their endowment, and actually received the keys of the kingdom of God, and oracles of God, keys of revelation, and the pattern of heavenly things; and thus addressing the Twelve, exclaimed, 'upon your shoulders the kingdom rests, and you must round up your shoulders, and bear it; for I have had to do it until now. But now the responsibility rests upon you. It mattereth not what becomes of me.'" (See Wilford Woodruff, Letter, *"To The Church of Jesus Christ of Latter-day Saints,"* the ***Times and Seasons***, Vol. 5 [Saturday, November 2, 1844], pp. 698–699; and *"Affidavit of Bathsheba W. Smith,"* cited in Smith, *"Joseph Smith Conferred All Keys on All the Twelve,"* ***Doctrines of Salvation***, Vol. 3, pp. 154–155).

64. In an address entitled *"The Right and Authority of President Brigham Young,"* presented in the Tabernacle in Salt Lake City, on Sunday afternoon, December 5, 1869, President George Q. Cannon said:

> "Previous to his death, the Prophet Joseph manifested great anxiety to see the temple completed . . . 'Hurry up the work, brethren,' he used to say, 'let us finish the temple; the Lord has a great endowment in store for you, and I am anxious that the brethren should have their endowments and receive the fullness of the Priesthood.' He urged the Saints forward continually, preaching unto them the importance of completing that building, so that therein the ordinances of life and salvation might be administered to the whole people . . . 'then,' said he, 'the Kingdom will be established, and I do not care what shall become of me.'
>
> ***"These were his expressions oft repeated in the congregations of the Saints, telling the brethren and sisters of the Church, and the world that he rolled the Kingdom on to the Twelve,*** and they would have to round up their shoulders and bear it off, as he was going to rest for awhile, and many other expressions of a like nature, the full meaning of which the Saints did not realize at the time." (Reported by John Grimshaw, as cited in ***Journal of Discourses,*** Vol. 13, p. 49, italics added).

"arose lion-like . . . and led the people forth from the region of death, to this desert and poorly land."[65]

Mantle of the Prophet Joseph Fell upon Brigham Young

Most present had not turned away their attention from the wagon where Sidney Rigdon had just concluded his remarks, but when Brigham Young began to speak, they "wheeled around and faced him, turning their backs upon Sidney Rigdon."[66] John Pulsipher recalled that "the very moment I heard him

65. Of these events, Mosiah Lyman Hancock also testified that "Brigham Young . . . lead the people forth from the region of death, to this desert and poorly land. Here he has caused the desert to blossom as the rose, according to the word of Holy Prophets . . . I remember Sidney Rigdon in his great desire to become Guardian of the Church. But I had seen the Prophet proclaim these words before the people, 'I have carried Sidney Rigdon long enough—I now throw him from my shoulders. If my brother Hyrum wishes to pick him up and carry him, he may—I carry him no longer." ("*Life Story of Mosiah Lyman Hancock*," compiled by his daughters, Amy E. Baird, Victoria H. Jackson, and Laura L. Wassell; Typescript, 1965, L. Tom Perry Special Collections, Harold B. Lee Library, Brigham Young University, p. 23, 30, 31).

Mosiah Lyman Hancock was born on Wednesday, April 9, 1834, in Kirtland, Ohio, the eldest of six sons and two daughters born to Levi Ward Hancock and Clarissa Reed Hancock. His parents were members of the Church, and his father had been ordained a Seventy and called as one of the first seven Presidents in February 1835. His family moved to Far West, Missouri and, after the persecutions there, on to Nauvoo. There he was acquainted with the Prophet, chopped wood with him, played "ball" with him and witnessed "remarkable" healings under the Prophet's hand. He was baptized April 10, 1842 by John Taylor, witnessed the Prophet's departure for Carthage and the return of his body after the Martyrdom. He traveled with his father's family to the Salt Lake Valley, lived near Warm Springs, was ordained a Seventy in 1852, and developed gardens and orchards. He later moved to Payson, fought in the Black Hawk war, assisted with the resistance to Johnston's Army in 1857, and eventually settled in southern Utah where he served in the St. George Temple, acting as a proxy for two signers of the Declaration of Independence on Friday, August 24, 1877. He then moved to Hubbard, Graham County, Arizona, where he died Monday, January 14, 1907.

66. Cannon, ***The Juvenile Instructor***, Vol. 22 (October 29, 1870), pp. 174–5, 182. In

speak (August 8th) I thought of Joseph."[67] Zerah Pulsipher

---

his address at a stake conference in Tooele, (as already noted—see footnotes #24 and #52 above), President Cannon testified: "After Sidney Rigdon had spoken, President Young arose and addressed the congregation, which faced around to see and hear him, turning their backs towards the wagon occupied by Sidney. Now it is probable that there are some here today who were present on that occasion, and they . . . could . . . bear witness that the power of God was manifested . . . But no sooner did President Young arise than the power of God rested down upon him . . . It did not appear to be Brigham Young; it appeared to be Joseph Smith that spoke to the people—Joseph in his looks, in his manner, and in his voice; even his figure was transformed so that it looked like that of Joseph, and everybody present, who had the Spirit of God, saw that he was the man whom God had chosen to hold the keys now that the Prophet Joseph had gone behind the veil, and that he had given him power to exercise them." Then President Cannon testified, "and from that time forward, notwithstanding the claims of Sidney Rigdon; notwithstanding the claims of Strang, notwithstanding the claims of William Smith, John E. Page and others who drew off from the Church in the days of Nauvoo; and notwithstanding the claims of other men who have since drawn off from the Church and made great pretensions, God has borne testimony to the acts and teachings of His servant Brigham, and those of his servants, the Apostles, who received the keys in connection with him. God sustained him and upheld him, and he blessed all those that listened to his counsel. No man that ever obeyed all his counsels and teachings was ever cursed, but was always blessed of God; while those who disobeyed his counsel did not prosper. We have all seen this." (Cannon, *"Joseph's Legal Successor," **Journal of Discourses***, Vol. 23, pp. 363–364).

67. John Pulsipher recalled that "after the death of the Prophet Joseph, Sidney Rigdon came and sought to place himself at the head of the Church. By his flatteries he deceived many. Just before he called a vote of the public congregation, Brigham Young, the President of the Twelve, arrived from his mission. This was a joyful meeting. The faithful knew not that Joseph had ordained Brother Brigham and the Twelve to lead the Church but they knew that the Twelve were the next quorum in authority. They that served the Lord faithful were not deceived. I went to meeting where the Church met in the grove east of the Temple where President Young arose and spoke and behold he spoke with the voice of Joseph. The very moment I heard him speak (August 8th) I thought of Joseph and from that time on his voice sounded like Joseph's and from that time the Church generally were satisfied that the mantle of Joseph was on Brigham." (John Pulsipher, *"Autobiography,"* Typescript, L. Tom Perry Special Collections, Harold B. Lee Library, Brigham Young University, pp. 7–8).

John Pulsipher was born in Spafford, Onondago County, New York, Tuesday, July 17, 1827, the second son and sixth child of Zerah Pulsipher (see note #64 below) and Mary Brown. As a child, he first became acquainted with the Prophet Joseph at

remembered that "Sidney made his plea." And then "Brigham Young began to speak and at that time I sat with my back towards the Stand as did many others. When Brigham spoke he spoke with the voice of Joseph and we turned around to see Brigham speaking in Joseph's voice . . ."[68] At that moment, the mantle, and the spirit and power of the Prophet Joseph Smith, fell visibly upon Brigham Young. Drusilla Hendricks "jumped up to look and see if it was not Brother Joseph."[69] George Q. Cannon, a

---

Kirtland, Ohio, in 1835. He was baptized Sunday, July 19, 1835, observed the apostasy in Kirtland, and traveled with the Kirtland Camp (the poorest Saints) to Adam-ondi-Ahman in Missouri. He moved with his family to Quincy, Illinois, and later, to Nauvoo, where he assisted in construction of the Temple and served in the Nauvoo Legion. He was present in the meeting on Thursday, August 8, 1844. He was ordained a Seventy, endowed in 1846, and assisted with the exodus. He eventually settled in Utah's Dixie, and died in Hebron, Washington County, Sunday, August 9, 1891.

68. Zerah Pulsipher, *"Autobiography,"* Typescript, L. Tom Perry Special Collections, Harold B. Lee Library, Brigham Young University, p. 20. Zerah Pulsipher was born June 24, 1789, at Rockingham, Windham County, Vermont. He was baptized January 11, 1832, moved to Kirtland, Ohio, was ordained an Elder and served missions in the eastern United States and Upper Canada in 1833-34 and 1837, baptizing, among many others, Wilford Woodruff, fourth President of the Church. He was a member of Zion's Camp, and moved to Daviess County, Missouri, where, in 1838, he was ordained and set apart as President of the First Quorum of Seventy. He left Missouri in 1839, settled in Nauvoo, assisted with the work of the Seventy there, and was present at the meeting on Thursday, August 8, 1844. He was endowed in 1845, and moved with the Saints to Utah, as captain of one of the pioneer companies, in 1848. He was released as a President of the Seventy in 1862 for misuse of the sealing power, but after review by the First Presidency, he was re-baptized and ordained a High Priest that same year. Subsequently, he was ordained a Patriarch and served until his death at Hebron, Washington County, Utah, in 1872 at the age of 83. (See Lyndon W. Cook, *"Zerah Pulsipher,"* ***Revelations of the Prophet Joseph Smith: Historical and Biographical Commentary of the Doctrine and Covenants*** [Originally Published by Seventy's Mission Bookstore, Provo, Utah; then in Salt Lake City: Deseret Book Company, 1982], pp. 270-271).

69. Drusilla Hendricks recalled that it "was not long before Sidney Rigdon called a meeting in order to present his claims to the Presidency . . . Some of the Twelve had returned . . . Brigham Young . . . and others, slipped up to the stand and said nothing

lad of seventeen at the time but later a Counselor in the First Presidency to four Presidents of the Church, declared that

> *". . . it was the voice of Joseph himself; and not only was it the voice of Joseph which was heard, but it seemed in the eyes of the people as though it was the very person of Joseph which stood before them. They both saw and heard with their natural eyes and ears, and then the words which were uttered came, accompanied by the convincing power of God, to their hearts, and they were filled with the Spirit and with great joy."*[70]

---

until Sidney Rigdon was through; he was standing . . . in a wagon . . . Then Pres. Brigham Young began to speak. I jumped up to look and see if it was not Brother Joseph for surely it was his voice and gestures. Every Latter-day Saint could easily see upon whom the priesthood descended for Brigham Young held the keys." (Drusilla Hendricks, "*A Historical Sketch,*" Church Historical Department, Salt Lake City, p. 26).

Drusilla Dorris Hendricks was born Thursday, February 8, 1810, the last of ten children born in a staunch Baptist family, spent her early years in Sumner County, Tennessee, suffered an extended illness as a child, and ascribed her recovery to the prayers of her parents. At the age of 18, on Thursday, May 31, 1827, she married James Hendricks, also the last in a family of ten children, of Simpson County, Kentucky. They joined the Church in Tennessee in 1835, and moved from Tennessee to Missouri. She found new strength from observing the Word of Wisdom, and said of her first years in Missouri that she "was never happier in her life." But troubles came—her husband was wounded in the Battle of Crooked River, and remained an invalid for life. She supported the family of five children by taking in washing and by knitting. They moved with the Church to Nauvoo, where she was present in the meeting at the Stand on Thursday, August 8, 1844. In the move west, she surrendered her eldest son, who was her greatest support, to service in the Mormon Battalion. The Hendricks family arrived in the Salt Lake Valley on Monday, October 4, 1847, and ten days later, her eldest son arrived with members of the Battalion from the west. They lived thirteen years in Salt Lake City, at Warm Springs, where they operated a bath house, and then in 1860 moved to Richmond in Cache County, Utah. At the time of her death, in Richmond, Friday, May 20, 1881, she had 67 grandchildren and 23 great-grandchildren. (Drusilla Hendricks, "*A Historical Sketch*").

70. Cannon in ***The Juvenile Instructor***, October 29, 1870, Vol. 22, pp. 174–175. The issue, for those well informed, was whether the Restoration had perished with the

Wilford Woodruff, himself a later successor to Brigham Young under the order of Apostolic Succession, was, in the forenoon of that windy August day, seated on the Stand near Brigham Young when Brigham arose to announce that the assembly originally scheduled for the following Tuesday would instead be convened that very afternoon. President Woodruff recalled that "if I had not seen him with my own

---

Prophet Joseph Smith, or whether the keys and powers, authorities and privileges, would continue. In an address on this question, presented in the Tabernacle in Salt Lake City, on Sunday, September 9, 1877, just eleven days following the death of President Brigham Young, Elder Erastus Snow, who was ordained an Apostle in 1849, and served as a member of the Quorum of the Twelve until his death in 1888, explained:

> "We have often heard our late President, Brigham Young, who was President of the Twelve Apostles by seniority, and who had been placed there by the voice of his brethren, to preside over his quorum, which had also been confirmed by the Lord, say that he was attending a Conference in Petersboro, New Hampshire, when he heard of the Prophet's death. The query arose in his mind: Where now rests those keys of the holy Priesthood which the Prophet Joseph received and revealed unto us . . . The answer came to him by the Holy Spirit resting upon him with a power and influence and peaceful assurance which caused him to bring his hand to his thigh with the utterance, 'They are here. They are here!' The voice of his brethren responded, and the echo reverberated . . . among . . . all the people. They are here, with brother Brigham, with his brethren the Apostles . . . This revelation of the Spirit to our beloved President, Brigham Young, on that occasion, and which also rested upon his brethren . . . was not a fresh call, a new revelation, but . . . bringing to their minds one . . . that had been spoken unto them through the Prophet Joseph . . . the charge that he gave to them to bear off the work which now rested upon their shoulders. ***From that day until the present time has this revelation been clear and prominent before the people, and in their hearts . . . How often has*** [Brigham Young] ***said, 'Joseph is still my leader; he is still my President; he still bears the keys before me. I am still following after him to carry out his counsel, to accomplish the work of which he laid the foundation, under God . . .'***
>
> "But the Lord signifies to me that these Quorums of the Priesthood shall go forward in their respective spheres of labor, and ***as one passes beyond the veil, following his file leader, the next Apostle will follow after, treading, as it were, in his footsteps, to bear off this kingdom.*** The work is of God and

eyes, there is no one who could have convinced me that it was not Joseph Smith, and anyone can testify to this who was acquainted with these two men."[71]

---

not of man, and no number of martyrdoms or death, and no amount of persecution nor slaying of the Lord's anointed, can put a stop to it . . . and that, if one passes beyond the veil, another follows in his footsteps . . . These utterances have often been made in our hearing, within the last thirty-three years, since the death of the Prophet Joseph, and have become household words with those who have been alive to their calling and duties, and whose eyes and ears have been open to hear the word of the Lord and remember it. ***How calm and peaceful the spirit and feelings of Israel on this memorable occasion, when our beloved President, who has led . . . for the last thirty-three years . . . was gathered to his fathers. How different was the spirit and feelings of Israel on this occasion from the other occasion I have referred to . . . It shows to our minds the education of the people, and their advancement in understanding and faith*** . . . In . . . all the Stakes of Zion, and in every department of our labor, there seems scarcely a ripple upon the smooth surface of the waters. Last Sabbath, when a vast congregation of the people came from the east, west, north and south, and from this city and its suburbs, to pay their last respects . . . the order, the silent and discreet feeling of resignation and peace that prevailed, should be a lesson to the Saints and a testimony to the world of the purity of faith that we have embraced, and the influence that had been exerted upon the hearts of the people by our departed leader . . . We find no confusion, no running to and fro . . . When we had finished the last sad rites . . . we found every one, on Monday morning, resuming his duties . . . The Saints everywhere, as well as our Elders abroad, move forward in the discharge of their duties with calmness and serenity, with assurance that Brigham is still our leader . . . but not on this side of the veil—he has gone into another sphere, to engage in the labors . . . with Joseph, Hyrum, and all the holy ones that have gone before in this dispensation, to assist them . . . while ***his brethren on this side of the veil tread softly and diligently after him, as it were in his footsteps,*** to move on the cause of Israel, and send the Gospel to the ends of the earth."(*"The Quorums of the Priesthood Will Continue to Go Forward—The Saints Are Calm and Undisturbed,"* reported by Rudger Clawson, in ***Journal of Discourses***, Vol. 19, pp. 102–103, italics added.

71. In the ***Deseret Evening News***, March 12, 1892; also cited in Smith, *"Twelve Apostles Accepted as the Presidency of the Church, Brigham Young at Their Head,"* ***History of the Church***, Vol. 7, p. 236.

In his diary, under the date of Thursday, August 8, 1844, Brigham Young noted that at the end of Sidney Rigdon's speech,

"I arose and spoke to the people, my heart was swollen with compassion toward them and by the power of the Holy

---

Orson Hyde, called as one of the first Apostles in 1835 and served as President of the Quorum from 1847 until 1877, probably returned to Nauvoo only the day of the meeting at the Stand, perhaps the day prior, and was present in the congregation. In an address in the 39th Semi-annual General Conference, he recalled: "I know that when President Young returned with the Twelve to Nauvoo, he gathered them around him, and said he, 'I want you to disperse among the congregation and feel the pulse of the people, while I go upon the stand and speak.' We went among the congregation and President Young went on the stand. Well, he spoke, and his words went through me like electricity. 'Am I mistaken?' said I, 'or is it really the voice of Joseph Smith?' This is my testimony; it was not only the voice of Joseph, but there were the features, the gestures and even the stature of Joseph before us in the person of Brigham . . . Every one in the congregation . . . inspired by the Spirit of the Lord . . . felt it. They knew it." Then President Hyde noted: "I sat myself down in the midst of the congregation, with my two wives, whom Joseph had given and sealed to me. When President Young began to speak, one of them said, 'It is the voice of Joseph! It is Joseph Smith!' The exclamation of the other was, 'I do not see him, where is he?' Well, the thought occurred to my mind respecting the Scripture which President Young has just quoted—'My sheep know my voice and follow me.' Where is the one that recognized the voice of Joseph in President Young? Where is she? She is in the line of her duty. But where is the other? Gone where I wish she were not. The sheep of the good shepherd will follow the voice they know, but they will not follow the voice of a stranger. Now this was a manifestation of the power of the Almighty . . . resting on an individual in the eyes of all the people, not only in feature and voice, but actually in stature. This is my testimony . . . Did it require argument to prove that brother Brigham Young held the position of Joseph, the martyred Prophet? Did it require proof that Joseph was there in the person of Brigham . . . It required no argument; ***with those who feared God and loved truth, it required none***." (At the Tabernacle in Salt Lake City, Wednesday, October 6, 1869, reported by John Grimshaw, cited as *"Right to Lead the Church,"* ***Journal of Discourses***, Vol. 13, p. 181, italics added).

Some years later, in an address at the 47th Annual General Conference, convened in conjunction with dedicatory services for the St. George Temple, President Orson Hyde affirmed:

"At the time our Prophet and Patriarch were killed . . . soon afterwards,

Ghost, even the spirit of the prophets, I was enabled to comfort the hearts of the Saints."[72]

The Testimony of the Saints

Wilford Woodruff left a record, as did William Carter Staines, Seymour Bicknell Young and others, that the transformation of Brigham Young, when he appeared to look like Joseph in stature, height, manner and gesture, and even to speak in the Prophet's voice, was observed by "hundreds" and even "thousands."[73]

Nancy Naomi Tracy, an early convert to the Church who returned to Nauvoo with her husband from a mission to New

---

when the Twelve returned to Nauvoo . . . we had a meeting . . . On his [Brigham Young] rising to speak, and as soon as he opened his mouth, I heard the voice of Joseph through him, and it was as familiar to me as the voice of my wife, the voice of my child, or the voice of my father. And not only the voice of Joseph did I distinctly and unmistakably hear, but I saw the very gestures of his person, the very features of his countenance, and if I mistake not, the very size of his person appeared on the stand. And ***it went through me with the thrill of conviction that Brigham was the man to lead this people.*** And from that day to the present there has not been a . . . doubt upon my mind with regard to the divinity of his appointment; I know that he was the man selected of God to fill the position he now holds." (At the Temple in St. George, on Thursday morning, April 5, 1877, reported by George F. Gibbs, cited as *"Prophet Joseph Manifest in Brigham,"* ***Journal of Discourses,*** Vol. 19, p. 59, italics added).

72. Diary of Brigham Young, August 8, 1844.

73. See, for example, Wilford Woodruff, *"Comprehensiveness of Latter-day Work,"* in the 42nd Annual General Conference, presented in the Tabernacle in Salt Lake City, Utah, Monday, April 8, 1872, reported by David W. Evans, in ***Journal of Discourses,*** Vol. 15, pp. 80–81; Seymour Bicknell Young, *"Brigham Young,"* from an address in an afternoon "overflow" session of the 92nd Semi-annual General Conference, in the Assembly Hall in Salt Lake City, Sunday afternoon, October 8, 1922, cited in ***Conference Report,*** October 1922, p. 146; and ***Journal of William C. Staines,*** August 8, 1844, in the *"Settlement of Church Leadership—Twelve Apostles Accepted as Presidency of Church, Brigham Young At Their Head,"* Smith, ***History of the Church,*** Vol. 7, p. 231,

York just in time to be present at the Stand at the grove that Thursday morning, August 8, 1844,[74] recorded:

> *"I can testify that the mantle of Joseph fell upon Brigham that day as that of Elijah did fall upon Elisha, for it seemed that his voice, his gestures, and all were Joseph. It seemed that we had him again with us. He [Brigham Young] was sustained by the voice of the people to be the prophet, seer, and revelator."*

"I was in the congregation," Benjamin Ashby would later testify, "when the form, voice and countenance of Brigham

---

footnote, p. 236; also cited in B. H. Roberts, *"Confusion—Choosing a Leader,"* ***Rise and Fall of Nauvoo***, pp. 328–329; Francis M. Gibbons, *"Order Out of Chaos,"* ***Brigham Young: Modern Moses, Prophet of God*** (Salt Lake City: Deseret Book Company, 1981), p. 104; and *"Introduction,"* ***Lion of the Lord: Essays on the Life and Service of Brigham Young***, ed. Susan Easton Black and Larry C. Porter (Salt Lake City: Deseret Book Company, 1995), p. ix. (Compare footnote #76 below).

74. Nancy Naomi Alexander Tracy was born in New York in 1816, married Moses Tracy in 1832, and was introduced to the Gospel by David W. Patten, the first President of the Twelve. She, with her husband, was baptized in 1834, relocated to Kirtland in 1835, was privileged to participate in the remarkable outpouring of the Spirit at the dedication of the Kirtland Temple, relocated again to Far West in 1837, watched her husband march off to the battle of Crooked River and return, and then relocated under threat of the mob from Missouri to Nauvoo in 1839. She attended the capstone ceremony for the Nauvoo Temple. She accompanied her husband on a mission to New York to advance the political candidacy of the Prophet. Upon learning of the Martyrdom, they returned to Nauvoo, arriving just in time for the meeting of Thursday, August 8, of which she wrote: "Our house had been rented while we were away. As soon as we arrived, we went right home and prepared to go to meeting for that day was appointed for us to choose a First Presidency to lead the Church. The Saints convened in the grove. Sidney Rigdon and his followers were on hand to contest their right to be the leaders of the Saints. At one time he was one of Brother Joseph's counselors, but he was not righteous, and Joseph shook him off saying that he had carried him long enough and he would carry him no longer. Therefore, it was

Young was transfigured before the congregation so that he appeared like Joseph Smith in every particular. The Lord showed

---

out of the question to have such a man lead the people. Brigham Young was the man chosen and sustained by unanimous vote to be the mouthpiece of God to the Saints. I can testify that the mantle of Joseph fell upon Brigham that day as that of Elijah did fall upon Elisha, for it seemed that his voice, his gestures, and all were Joseph. It seemed that we had him again with us. He [Brigham Young] was sustained by the voice of the people to be the prophet, seer, and revelator," ("*Autobiography*," Typescript, L. Tom Perry Special Collections, Harold B. Lee Library, Brigham Young University, p. 31). Subsequently, they traveled with the Saints to Utah where she spent the remainder of her life. In 1880, at the age of 64, she concluded her autobiography: "what I have written is true . . . I am now 64 years old and I have lived in this Church 46 of those years and am sure that eternal life will be my reward if I am firm to the end." ("*Nancy Naomi Tracy Autobiography*," Typescript, Mormon Collection, Bancroft Library, University of California at Berkeley, p. 36. Compare "*Reminiscences and Diary of Nancy Naomi Alexander Tracy*," Typescript, Church Historical Department). She died at Marriott, in Weber County, Utah, on Tuesday, March 11, 1902, at the age of 85.

Ezra T. Clark recorded a testimony consistent with those previously cited. He noted that when "Brigham Young arose as leader of the Church, I want to bear record that he spoke as Joseph used to speak; to all appearances, the same voice, the same gestures, the same stature." ("*Testimony and Instructions*," ***The Improvement Era***, Vol. 5 [January 1901], pp. 200–202).

Ezra T. Clark was born in Lawrence, Illinois, Sunday, November 23, 1823, was acquainted with the Prophet Joseph Smith in Nauvoo, was in Nauvoo after the Martyrdom to witness the succession of Brigham Young, traveled with the Saints to Utah in 1848 and settled in Farmington, Davis County, Utah, where he prospered, eventually contributing to a number of philanthropic causes. He was named President of the 40th Quorum of Seventy which was organized at Farmington in 1855, and subsequently served several missions, one to England, in 1856, where he met the woman who would later become his second wife in plural marriage. He was arrested for that practice in 1886 by Federal marshals and after a trial was fined $300 and sentenced to six months in prison. He was an intimate friend of President Wilford Woodruff. He died in Farmington on Thursday, October 17, 1901.

At the 68th Semi-annual General Conference, Heber J. Grant, who became the sixth successor of the Prophet Joseph Smith, testified: "I know the mantle of Joseph Smith fell upon the Prophet Brigham Young . . . I know it because my mother, a more honest woman than whom never lived, a more devoted Latter-day Saint can not be found; because she and scores of others have told me that they saw the Prophet Brigham Young when he spoke with the voice of Joseph Smith; when he looked like

the people that the mantle of [the Prophet] Joseph had been bestowed upon Brigham."[75] Susa Young Gates, one of the daughters of Brigham Young, who with Leah Widtsoe interviewed many of those who were eyewitness to this

---

the Prophet Joseph; and I know that these people are honest." (At the Tabernacle in Salt Lake City, on Friday afternoon, October 7, 1898, cited as *"The Church Perpetuated," **Conference Report***, October, 1898, p. 36).

75. Benjamin Ashby noted that after the Martyrdom, "the grief and sorrow of a whole people cannot be pictured in language; for days, a man, woman or child could not be met but they were in tears for the loss of their beloved leader. Soon the wagons containing the two brothers arrived in the city and passed down to the Mansion House where we visited and viewed their marred features . . . Sidney Rigdon endeavored to have himself elected as guardian of the Church and I was present when he made his silly and boastful speech about leading the Church. [He spoke of traveling] Back to Pittsburgh and [about] the nose of Queen Victoria, etc., etc. Too foolish to be worth remembering. I did not know Rigdon when he was in the spirit of his calling and cannot say what manner of man he was, but when I knew him he had lost the favor of God and he was as dry as sticks in his preaching." ("*Autobiography*," pp. 10–11; brackets added, compare footnote #43 above).

The Prophet had escaped from his enemies many times before. The Saints had not imagined the Church without Joseph, and had reason to expect that he might live to an advanced age. (See D&C 130:14). They had no prior experience with succession. At the 79th Semi-annual General Conference, Elder Orson F. Whitney, who was ordained an Apostle on Monday, April 9, 1906 and served as a member of the Quorum until his death in 1931, declared:

> "I presume this question arose during the lifetime of the prophet Joseph Smith, the first President of the Church. Doubtless many of the Latter-day Saints then asked themselves the question, 'What would we do if the Prophet were taken away? Where would we find another president, another leader?' The Prophet seemed absolutely indispensable to his generation; but when the Lord saw fit to take him, another man arose-up to that time not noted, any more than several of the brethren with whom he was associated. He was a mighty man, and they were mighty men. But when the mantle of Joseph fell upon him, when God had chosen Brigham Young to be His prophet, and the Saints had sustained him with the uplifted hand and with the power of their faith and prayers, as their president, where was the man in all Israel who could compare with President Brigham Young . . . God chose Brigham Young and placed the power of presidency upon him. That was the secret of his

transformation and co-authored a major biography of Joseph's successor, reported that her father, in that moment, was "clothed with the very appearance, the very voice and manner of the martyred Prophet. The people, 'thousands' of them,[76] bore

---

might—the secret of his success. This is the Lord's work, and it is the Lord who makes His servants mighty. When President Young drew near to his end, many were asking themselves the question: who will take his place? Where is there another man of his sagacity, his wisdom, his executive ability? Brigham Young had made himself almost indispensable to the Latter-day Saints, and in the world, among the Gentiles, speculation was rife, and predictions were numerous . . . that when Brigham Young died Mormonism would be at an end . . . There was no confusion. There may have been some question as to who was qualified to take the place of Brigham Young at the head of the Church; but when John Taylor had been sustained as President, when the people had united their prayers in his behalf, and God had clothed him with the power of the presidency, it was perfectly apparent to the Latter-day Saints that another leader had been provided, and that he, from that time, would be the strongest and mightiest man among them.

"It was the same when President Taylor died; it was the same when President Woodruff died; and when President Snow passed away, the man for the time and place was found; as he always will be. It is the Lord's business to find him and to qualify him for His work; and the Lord has never failed. This is my testimony concerning all the leaders of Israel including our honored and beloved President Joseph F. Smith." (At the Tabernacle in Salt Lake City, on Monday afternoon, October 4, 1909, cited as *"God Finds and Qualifies His Servants—The Power of Presidency,"* ***Conference Report,*** October 1909, pp. 85–86, italics added).

76. William Carter Staines noted that "I thought it was he and so did ***thousands*** who heard it." (See ***The Journal of William C. Staines***, August 8, 1844, as cited in "*Settlement of Church Leadership,*" Smith, ***History of the Church***, Vol. 7, p. 231, footnote, p. 236. Compare footnote #73 above.

William Carter Staines was born Saturday, September 26, 1818, at Higham Ferries, Northhamptonshire, England. The family moved to Beddenham, near Bedford, about 40 miles from London. He suffered an accident on the ice at age 13 which injured and deformed his spine and left him in pain for the remainder of his life. He worked in his father's truck garden. In 1841, at the age of 23, he joined the Church, served as a missionary in England, was closely associated with President Lorenzo Snow there, and then removed to Nauvoo, where he was introduced to the Prophet Joseph Smith,

witness to this event then and in after years. 'It is Joseph!' they whispered to each other, many of them weeping as they looked and listened."[77]

The Witness Was Not Momentary But Enduring

This divine witness, that the Prophetic mantle now rested upon Brigham Young, was not fleeting, but apparently was manifest in his speech, and even his appearance, through a period of several weeks, and perhaps longer. Just a few days after the October conference that year, two full months after the special witness of Thursday, August 8 was first observed,

---

whom he recognized instantly, having seen him in a vision while crossing the sea. He worked on construction of the Nauvoo Temple and was in St. Louis on Temple business when he learned of the Martyrdom. He wrote that "the grief and sorrow of the . . . Saints was heartfelt . . . the mourning of a community of many thousands, all of whom revered these martyred brethren . . . the whole people wept in going to and from the scene—all, all were weeping." He attended the meeting at the Stand on Thursday, August 8, 1844. On the plains, he tarried with the Ponca tribe, learned their dialect and taught them the Gospel. In February, 1847, he rejoined the Saints and traveled to the Great Salt Lake Valley, arriving on Wednesday, September 15, 1847. As an expert gardener, he cultivated fruits and flowers upon his own properties in Salt Lake and a 300 acre farm in Davis County, and superintended many of the gardens and orchards belonging to President Brigham Young. He served as the Territorial Librarian, on a posse to guard the Overland Mail route, in Echo Canyon in 1857, and for a period on the Salt Lake City Council. As a founding partner of Staines, Needham and Company, he prospered. Leaving the day to day operations of his business in the care of others, he served a mission to Ireland from 1860 until 1863, and then served as an emigration agent for the Church, spending the better part of each year in New York City and then returning to Utah only in the Winter months, from 1863 until his death on Wednesday, August 3, 1881. Having no children, he provided first for his wives, and then left the remainder of his substantial estate to the Church. (See Andrew Jenson, *"William Carter Staines,"* ***LDS Biographical Encyclopedia: A Compilation of Biographical Sketches of Prominent Men and Women in The Church of Jesus Christ of Latter-day Saints***, 4 Volumes, 1st Edition [Salt Lake City: Andrew Jenson History Company, 1914], Vol. 2, pp. 513–518).

77. Gates and Widtsoe, ***Life Story of Brigham Young***, pp. 40–41.

an unnamed correspondent to the ***Times and Seasons*** boldly inquired, expressing the sentiments of many:

> *"It has been remarked by some that we would be broken up, scattered, thrown into confusion and disorder [after losing] our Prophet . . . but I think that those who were present at our late conference found that it was not so. When, I would ask, was there ever a greater unanimity of feeling, better order, a greater disposition among the Saints to do the will of God than on this occasion? I say never . . . Who can't see that* **the mantle of the Prophet** *(using a figure)* **has fallen on President Young and the Twelve?** *Who can't see that the* **same spirit which inspired our beloved brother Joseph Smith, now inspires President Young** *. . . I am satisfied that the Saints who were present, all felt that God is with us, and that God is with the Twelve . . .* **I am well satisfied that we as a people have nothing to fear. We are in the hands of God and He will take care of us.** *We will thank Him for past mercies, and trust Him for the future . . ."*[78]

Joseph Grafton Hovey[79] recorded that as he approached Winter Quarters with his family, on the morning of Tuesday, September 1, 1846, (just over two years after that windy day in August, 1844, when the Prophet Joseph's mantle rested upon Brigham Young), as they "came near the ferry . . . Brother Brigham and Lorenzo . . . crossed the river to meet us." Brother

78. *"Communications,"* ***The Times and Seasons***, Vol. 5 (Tuesday, October 15, 1844), p. 675, italics and brackets added.

79. In an address in the Old Tabernacle in Great Salt Lake City, President Brigham

Hovey wrote that "I was pleased to see President Brigham Young after not seeing him for seven months. He looked very much like Brother Joseph, the Seer, so much so that at first sight I thought he was the Prophet Joseph."[80]

This testimony about a spirit or power that fell upon Brigham Young and continued to rest upon him throughout the course of his ministry is in harmony with a statement of Elder Albert Carrington,[81] who later served as a Counselor in

---

Young declared: "I wish we had in our midst thousands and millions of such men as Joseph Hovey." (*"Lawyers, and Those Who Practice Attending Law Courts, Rebuked—A Curse Pronounced upon All who Love Litigation and Do Not Repent,"* Sunday, February 24, 1856, as cited in ***Journal of Discourses***, Vol. 3, p. 240. Joseph Grafton Hovey was born on Tuesday, November 17, 1812, in Middlesex County, Massachusetts, the son of Thomas Hovey and Elizabeth Sever, was married to Martha Ann Webster of Portsmouth, New Hampshire in 1833, joined the Saints in Far West, and was baptized by William Draper, Thursday, July 4, 1839, during the flight of the Saints from Missouri. He labored as a stonecutter on the Nauvoo Temple, and buried his wife and five children in Iowa during the trek from Nauvoo to Winter Quarters. In 1846, he married Sarah Baily at Winter Quarters, and arrived in the Salt Lake Valley on Saturday, September 23, 1848. He settled his family in Salt Lake City, served as a counselor to Bishop Alonzo H. Raleigh in the 19th Ward, labored as a stonecutter on the Salt Lake Temple, and served a mission to southern Utah as a part of the general "reformation" that was undertaken throughout the Church in 1856, during the course of which he earned a reputation as "a most energetic and successful worker" and the admiration and approval of President Brigham Young. He married twice more: Sarah Goodridge in 1850 and Susannah Goodridge in 1852, and became the father of ten more children, moved to Cache Valley in 1860 which he helped to settle and became the first Bishop of the Millville Ward. He returned to Salt Lake City in 1863 where he continued his work as a stonecutter on the Salt Lake Temple and served there until his death on Wednesday, May 6, 1868, at Salt Lake City, at the age of 56. Compare Joseph Hovey, ***Autobiography of Joseph Grafton Hovey: 1812–1868***, Typescript, L. Tom Perry Special Collections, Harold B. Lee Library, Brigham Young University, Provo, Utah.

80. Joseph G. Hovey, *"Arrives at Council Bluffs, Winter Quarters,"* ***Autobiography***, p. 40, italics added.

81. Albert Carrington was born at Royalton, Windsor County, Vermont, on Friday, January 8, 1813. He graduated from Dartmouth College—now Dartmouth University in 1833, practiced law in Pennsylvania, operated a lead mine in Wisconsin, joined the

the First Presidency, that was reported by Brigham Young himself in 1857:

> *"Brother Carrington's testimony proves to you that men's eyes are liable to be deceived. It may appear strange to some that he could not tell me from Joseph Smith, when I was speaking in the Stand in Nauvoo during the October Conference of 1844. Somebody came along and passed a finger over his eyes and he could not see any one but Joseph speaking, until I got through addressing the congregation."*[82]

In that same address in 1857, President Brigham Young affirmed that "I may die for my religion . . . and the spirit of

---

Church in Wisconsin, gathered to Nauvoo, and was a member of the pioneer company that entered the Salt Lake Valley in July, 1847. He served as assessor in the provisional State of Deseret, as a member of Captain Howard Stansbury's party that surveyed the Great Salt Lake, as Editor of the Deseret News, as a member of the Utah territorial legislature, for more than twenty years as the Private Secretary to President Brigham Young, and in England as President of the European Mission. Upon his return to Utah at the conclusion of his mission, he was ordained an Apostle and served as a member of the Quorum of the Twelve from Sunday, July 3, 1870 until he was called to serve as a Counselor in the First Presidency to President Brigham Young, on Tuesday, April 8, 1873. He was released when the First Presidency was dissolved at the death of Brigham Young, on Wednesday, August 29, 1977, and served again in the Quorum of the Twelve. During his twenty years of service to Brigham Young, he had been entrusted by Brigham Young with many of his personal affairs, and labored for many years as one of the administrators appointed to settle President Young's estate. He returned three more times to England to preside over the European Mission. In 1879, with President George Q. Cannon, he was confined in the Utah penitentiary for refusing to post exorbitant bail demanded under the Edmunds bill. For personal transgression, he was excommunicated in 1885, but was baptized again in 1887, and died in Salt Lake City on Thursday, September 19, 1889).

82. President Brigham Young, *"Futile Efforts of the Enemy,"* from an address presented in the Bowery in Great Salt Lake City, Sunday, July 19, 1857, ***Journal of Discourses***, Vol. 5, pp. 57–58.

Joseph which fell upon me is ready to fall upon somebody else when I am removed."[83]

83. Ibid., p. 57.

Epilogue

Brigham Young spoke only briefly.[84] His purpose, in rising to speak at the morning meeting, was not to make a major address, but rather to call for the assembly of the Priesthood and members that had originally been appointed to meet the next Tuesday to convene instead that very afternoon, at 2:00 PM. With that announcement, together with some few remarks about how he would much rather have returned to Nauvoo and mourned thirty days for the dead prophet rather than attend so hastily to the

84. William Bryan Pace, after first noting that "Sidney Rigdon, Brigham Young and the twelve were absent [from Nauvoo] at the Prophet's death," then testified of the struggle that followed:

> "Sidney Rigdon spent, what seemed to me several hours, haranguing the people on the importance of making him their leader, after which, Brigham Young arose and said only a word, when it was observed by the whole congregation that the mantle of 'Joseph' was upon him, in word, gesture and general appearance." (William Bryan Pace, "*Autobiography*, 1832–1847," Typescript, L. Tom Perry Special Collections, Harold B. Lee Library, Brigham Young University, Provo Utah, p. 7. Compare footnote #107 below).

business of appointing a leader in Joseph's stead, Brigham Young dismissed the assembly.[85] The Saints dispersed quickly to their homes, "rejoicing" in anticipation of the assembly that would convene that afternoon. "Uncertainty and anxiety" were fled. "They had heard the voice of the shepherd at last."[86]

---

85. Jenson, ***The Historical Record,*** Vol. 7, pp. 789–791. Lyman Littlefield testified that "after Mr. Rigdon dismissed his meeting, Apostle Brigham Young arose and called the people to order. There seemed to be felt a general feeling of relief and all gladly kept their seats to listen to the new speaker, who stated very feelingly in substance that ***it was contrary to his wishes to so soon have to speak upon the matter of choosing a successor to our beloved Brother Joseph Smith, the Prophet, whom God had raised up to establish the great work of the last days. He felt like anointing his head, as did Aaron, and mourning for his brethren for thirty days in sackcloth and ashes,*** before entering upon the duty then forced upon him. He said Brother Rigdon seemed to be in a hurry about the matter and the course he had taken made it necessary that the people should come to an understanding and find out upon whom the mantle had fallen." (***Reminiscences of the Latter-day Saints*** [Logan: The Utah Journal Company, 1888], Chapter 2, pp. 165–166).

Lyman Omer Littlefield was born on Monday, November 22, 1819, in Verona Township, Oneida County, New York. He was baptized by Peter Whitmer in Clay County, Missouri, in 1834, and in that same year, although only thirteen years old, was a member of Zion's Camp. Suffering from feelings of melancholy one day, in the course of the march, he noted that the Prophet, although the "busiest man of the camp . . . yet when he saw me, he turned from the great press of other duties to say a word of comfort to a child. Placing his hand upon my head, he said, 'Is there no place for you, my boy? If not, we must make one.' This circumstance made an impression upon my mind which the long lapse of time and cares of riper years have not effaced." He moved with his father's family to Missouri where the family suffered in the persecutions there, and then to Nauvoo where he worked in the printing office of the ***Nauvoo Neighbor*** and the ***Times and Seasons***. From Nauvoo, he served a mission to Great Britain, accompanied a party of Saints from England to the Salt Lake Valley in 1848, and settled in Cache Valley in 1882. Continuing his interest in the printed word, he published ***The Martyrs: A Sketch of the Lives and a Full Account of the Martyrdom of Joseph and Hyrum Smith*** (Salt Lake City: Juvenile Instructor Office, 1882). He died Friday, September 1, 1893, at Smithfield, Cache County, Utah, at 74.

86. Jenson, ***The Historical Record,*** Vol. 7, pp. 789–791. While many diarists

By the time the afternoon meeting convened, the wind had picked up again. The course of the afternoon meeting is a matter of record,[87] when Brigham Young addressed the Saints

---

notice the apparent relief and happiness of the Saints in hearing Brigham Young speak briefly at the close of the morning meeting, and while a great many of them also record that they were eyewitness to the remarkable spirit and mantle evident in Brigham Young, yet there is little recorded notice of efforts made to assemble the Saints for the afternoon meeting, only record that the meeting was held that afternoon, and that the meeting was attended by "thousands." The Scriptures record that after Jesus's first appearance among the Nephites, after He had dismissed them: "go ye unto your homes, and ponder upon the things which I have said, and ask of the Father, in my name, that ye may understand, and prepare your minds for the morrow, and I come unto you again" (3 Nephi 17:3), there was an enormous effort to assemble as many as possible so that they would be at the Temple site the following day, at the place and at the time when Jesus had promised to return:

> "And it was noised abroad among the people immediately, before it was yet dark, that the multitude had seen Jesus, and that he had ministered unto them, and that he would also show himself on the morrow unto the multitude.
>
> "Yea, and even all the night it was noised abroad concerning Jesus; and insomuch did they send forth unto the people that there were many, yea, an exceedingly great number, did labor exceedingly all that night, that they might be on the morrow in the place where Jesus should show himself unto the multitude," (3 Nephi 19:2–3).

Perhaps the same yearnings may have inspired the efforts of faithful Saints during the interval between the morning meeting and the afternoon meeting, on that Thursday, August 8, 1844.

87. In the meeting on Wednesday, August 7, at 4:00 P.M., when Brigham Young announced plans for the assembly originally scheduled for Tuesday, August 13, he stated: "I want to see this people, with the various quorums of the priesthood, assembled together in special conference . . ." When Sidney Rigdon concluded his remarks, Brigham Young, according to the ***History of the Church***, gave out an appointment for the *brethren* to assemble at 2:00 PM. "At the appointed time the brethren came together. Present, of the Twelve, Brigham Young, Heber C. Kimball, Parley P. Pratt, Orson Pratt, Willard Richards, Wilford Woodruff, George A. Smith. The several quorums were organized on and around the stand according to order," (Smith, ***History of the Church***, Vol. 7, pp. 230–231). B. H. Roberts

for "about two hours in the open air with the wind blowing,"[88] when Sidney Rigdon subsequently declined to have his name presented,[89] and when the Quorum of the Twelve Apostles,

---

included a footnote at this point: "It will be observed that there were seven of the Apostles present, a majority of the Quorum. Of the absent ones, John Taylor was confined to his home, not yet recovered from his wounds, Orson Hyde, John E. Page, and Wm. Smith had not yet arrived in Nauvoo; and Lyman Wight was still in the east." It is true that John Taylor was still recovering and was, for the most part, confined at home, and appears not to have attended the meeting at the Stand on Thursday afternoon, August 8, 1844. But Orson Hyde testified that he was present in the meetings of that day (see footnote #71), while William Smith and John E. Page had not yet arrived at Nauvoo, (compare footnotes #23, #31, and #34 above). But it appears that Lyman Wight was in Nauvoo, and it is either an oversight that his name was not listed among those of the Twelve attending the afternoon meeting, or he was elsewhere in the city that afternoon.

On Monday, May 20, 1844, a meeting was convened "at the Stand for the purpose of collecting means to enable Elder Lyman Wight to go to Washington . . ." And on Tuesday, May 21, "Elders Brigham Young, Heber C. Kimball, Lyman Wight, and about a hundred Elders, left this city on the steamer *Osprey* [for] St. Louis" to fulfil their appointed missions to preach the gospel and advance the Prophet's candidacy for the presidency of the United States. A month later, when the Prophet was impressed that he would soon be taken, and that the Twelve should return to Nauvoo so they would be present to carry the burden of the kingdom in his absence, Elder Lyman Wight was in Baltimore, (Smith, ***History of the Church***, Vol. 6, pp. 398–399, 518). He then traveled to Boston where he labored alongside President Brigham Young, Heber C. Kimball, Orson Hyde, Orson Pratt, William Smith and Wilford Woodruff. When the brethren of the Twelve did receive word to return to Nauvoo, and confirmed the reports of the Martyrdom, they "were delayed in Boston several days, waiting upon Elder Lyman Wight to accompany them to Nauvoo." On Sunday, August 11, 1844, just three days after the meeting on Thursday, Lyman Wight preached at the Stand "about leading a company away into the wilderness," and on Wednesday, August 21, he was too sick to attend a meeting of the Twelve, (Smith, ***History of the Church***, Vol. 7, pp. 149, 209, 248, 261). So it appears that, although he left Nauvoo with others of the Twelve in May, he had returned with them by Wednesday, August 7, and participated in events there until his departure for Texas.

88. Diary of Brigham Young, Thursday, August 8, 1844.

89. When the afternoon meeting got underway, Brigham Young was the first to speak, stating that the Prophet Joseph Smith had conferred all of the keys and

with Brigham Young standing at their head, was sustained by all the quorums of the Priesthood, and by the members.

Now, dear reader, it is August 8, 1844, in Nauvoo. Our beloved Prophet leader has passed away. The Saints are like sheep without a shepherd. Who is to lead the Church? How can anyone know for sure? You have never really considered the doctrine of succession. How can you know that you will follow the Lord's appointed leader? You have no experience upon which to base your decision.[90] The crisis comes so

---

powers that he himself held upon the Twelve. He was followed by Amasa Lyman (see footnote #22 above) who supported the Twelve. Sidney Rigdon was then invited to speak, but he declined, and asked W. W. Phelps, a prominent Elder, to speak for him; Brother Phelps supported the Twelve. He was followed by Parley P. Pratt (see footnotes #31, #39 and #40) who spoke in support of the Twelve and admonished the Saints to stop trading with enemies of the Church. Then Brigham arose again to speak: "I want every man before he enters into a covenant, to know what he is going to do, but we want to know if this people will support the priesthood . . . If you say you will, do so." He was then about to put the question to the assembled quorums as to whether or not they wanted Sidney Rigdon for a leader, but at the request of Sidney Rigdon, Brigham first offered the question of whether the assembly would support the Twelve as the presiding quorum: "Do the church want and is their only desire to sustain the Twelve as the First Presidency of this people . . . If the Church want the Twelve to stand as the head, the First Presidency of the Church . . . every man, every woman, every quorum is now put in order, and you are now the sole controllers of it—all that are in favor . . . manifest it by holding up the right hand. (There was a universal vote.) If there are any of the contrary mind—every man, every woman, who does not want the Twelve to preside—lift up your hands in like manner. (No hands up). This supercedes the other question [whether Sidney Rigdon should preside], and trying it by quorums [allowing each quorum to vote separately] . . . This disposed of Sidney Rigdon's claims. He had full opportunity to present his case . . . The Saints had full opportunity and liberty to vote for him . . . but they rejected him and sustained the Twelve." (See Roberts, *"Choosing a Leader," **The Rise and Fall of Nauvoo***, Chapter 39, pp. 323–333, brackets added).

90. Elder Orson F. Whitney said of these events in Nauvoo in 1844: "A crisis had come. The First Presidency was no more. Death had dissolved that quorum.

suddenly. You feel that your decision this morning will be vital to your eternal progress. Sidney Rigdon has been venerated for many years as a Counselor to the Prophet Joseph Smith. He is speaking now; in a few moments he will complete his remarks and step down from the wagon. Brigham Young will then arise on the Stand behind you, to speak, but for only a few minutes. Some will know immediately, by the revelations of the Holy Ghost, that Brigham Young is to lead.

But will you know? Have you prepared yourself to know? Have you followed the counsel of Church leaders? Are you clean and worthy to have the still, small voice of the Spirit whisper assurance and peace and direction within your soul? Will you recognize the voice of authority? Will you be able to hear the voice of the true shepherd? Or will this meeting pass with you completely unaware that the Eternal God has again manifested His will? Sidney Rigdon is now finished. Brigham Young is just now standing up. This instant may be the most crucial in your opportunity for salvation and eternal blessings. Are you ready?

Next stood the Twelve, an independent body, now holding the keys of the kingdom, from Joseph, its earthly founder. But this fact, though known to the Apostles, upon whom he had rolled that burden and conferred that authority, was not so patent to the people. The order of the Priesthood was not so well known then as now." Then Elder Whitney stated: "Experience had not supplemented revelation on these points, and doubtless there were many Saints in Nauvoo, as there are many now, who were not informed upon things which had been plainly taught them for years. Besides, Sidney Rigdon, one of the three first presidents, was alive, to press his claims to the leadership, and not a few of the Saints openly favored his ambitious pretensions. Who was to decide in such a controversy, and how was the right man to be known ?" (*"One Having Authority," **Life of Heber C. Kimball,*** 3rd printing of a Lithographic Reprint of the 1888 Edition [Salt Lake City: Bookcraft, 1973], pp. 343–344).

For its effect upon the members of the Church, the import of the divine outpouring upon the Saints, in the morning meeting on Thursday, August 8, 1844, can scarcely be overestimated.[91] It is a powerful witness, that hundreds of the Saints testified of then and in later years, in diaries and journals, in sermons, and by their nodding assent as the event was described in sermons by others, that Brigham Young had indeed been transformed before them that morning—that he seemed to possess Joseph Smith's voice and gestures, and that, to many, it appeared that Joseph stood before them.

---

91. President Joseph Fielding Smith explained that Sidney Rigdon "assumed authority and stood forth before the people demanding their attention and claiming the right of presidency. The matter, however, was properly settled . . . and President Brigham Young, whose right it was, was sustained by the vote of the Latter-day Saints . . . And yet it became necessary on that occasion, while President Young was speaking to the people, before the vote was taken, for the Lord to make it known by a manifestation that he was indeed the successor of the Prophet Joseph and that the mantle of his predecessor had fallen upon his shoulders. Such a thing as that is not required today because now we have learned the order of the Church." (***Conference Report***, June, 1919, p. 93).

Elder Seymour Bicknell Young, nephew of Brigham Young and senior President of the First Council of the Seventy at the time, in a testimony presented when he was 85 years of age, declared similarly:

> "President Brigham Young after the martyrdom . . . in a large congregationon . . . in the grove . . . was endowed with power from on high . . . and ***hundreds and thousands of the Saints testified that they saw the mantle of Joseph fall upon the Prophet Brigham Young, and that Joseph's voice came from the lips of Brigham Young, and the power and the testimony of the Prophet was in his utterances***. It seems to me that something of this kind was necessary, because the people had become sorrowful after the martyrdom because of the many apostates that had sought to lead the Church astray, and this very providential manifestation seemed to satisfy the Saints. From that time they knew that Brigham Young was the prophet, seer, and revelator and President . . . and that the power of his prophetic ministry had been manifest," ("*Brigham Young,*" address in the afternoon "overflow" session of the 92nd

The keys of the kingdom of God, restored by the ministration of holy angels to the Prophet Joseph Smith, and conferred by him upon the members of the Twelve, with Brigham Young at their head, were still here! The keys were here on earth, the keys are here on earth; they will remain here.

"For unto you, the Twelve," the Lord had revealed through the Prophet Joseph Smith in July 1837, "and those, the First Presidency, who are appointed with you to be your counselors and your leaders, is the power of this priesthood given, for the last days and for the last time, in the which is the dispensation of the fulness of times . . .[92]

Semi-annual General Conference, in the Assembly Hall on Temple Square in Salt Lake City, Sunday afternoon, October 8, 1922, ***Conference Report***, October 1922, p. 146).

Seymour Bicknell Young was born Tuesday, October 3, 1837, in Kirtland, Ohio, a son of Joseph Young and Jane Adeline Bicknell, and nephew of Brigham Young. As a child, he was carried through a rain of bullets in his mother's arms at the massacre at Haun's Mill, Missouri in 1838. He lived in Nauvoo and although only a child, recalled the Prophet Joseph and the events which are the subject of this study. He was baptized in Carterville, Ohio, in 1848, in the course of his family's move west; and lived for three years in Pottawatamie County, Iowa, while his father had responsibilities at the Kanesville settlement to support the Mormon emigration. The Young family arrived in the Salt Lake Valley in September, 1850. He was among the first party to settle the Cache Valley, was ordained an Elder in the Endowment House, served a mission to Great Britain but was called home when Johnston's army threatened, continued military service with companies protecting the overland telegraph during the Civil War and in the Black Hawk War, and spent years grading railroad for the Union Pacific Railroad. He then pursued the study of medicine, graduated from the University Medical College of New York in 1874 and became a practicing physician. He was called to the First Council of Seventy Thursday, October 14, 1882, at age 45, becoming the senior President in 1893, and served in that capacity until his death in Salt Lake City, Utah, Monday, December 15, 1915, at the age of 77. (Jenson, "*Seymour Bicknell Young,*" ***LDS Biographical Encyclopedia***, Vol. 1, pp. 200–202).

92. D&C 112:30. This assurance was revealed to the Prophet Joseph on the day the Gospel was first preached in England, to instruct Thomas B. Marsh, the

Saints today may have the same witness, certain and sure, that the keys of the priesthood and presidency are here, and that the Lord's Prophet today acts under the authority of the same "mantle" that has rested upon all of the Lord's prophets in all ages of the world. President Wilford Woodruff, speaking as the successor to the Prophet Joseph Smith, after Brigham Young and John Taylor, as the fourth Prophet in the dispensation of the fulness of times, testified:

> *"I have never had any testimony since I have been in the flesh, that has been greater than the testimony of the Holy Ghost. That is the strongest testimony that can be given to me or to any man in the flesh. Now, every man has a right to that, and when he obtains it, it is a living witness to him. It deceives no man, and never has . . .*
>
> *"I say to you . . . the Kingdom of God is here. The Priesthood is here. The keys of the Kingdom of God are here. They will remain here. It makes no difference whether Joseph Smith, Brigham Young, John Taylor, Wilford Woodruff, or anybody else, remains; while these keys are here we have a right to know the mind and will of God; and when we do our duty, when we live our religion, we shall have these principles manifested to us. I know what awaits this nation. I know what awaits the Latter-day Saints. Many things have been shown to me by vision and by revelation . . . No matter if earth and hell combine against us, we are in His hands, and*

---

first President of the Quorum of the Twelve, and all who have held or now hold that sacred office, of their duty and responsibility, to admonish them to purify their hearts and press forward to open doors to preaching of the Gospel in all the world, at Kirtland, Ohio, Sunday, July 23, 1837, italics added.

He has said that He will guide and direct the affairs of the Kingdom. The Lord is no different today from what He was in the days of Adam, of Enoch, of Christ, of Joseph [Smith and] of Brigham [Young]. The Latter-day Saints should seek for the Spirit of God. We have great power and great blessings given unto us."[93]

These many accounts of the sacred assurance, poured out upon the heads of so many in the vast congregation of anxious Saints assembled at the Stand in the grove near the temple site on that windy day in August, in 1844, stand as one testimony, as one of the fundamental witnesses of the Restoration: that

---

93. President Wilford Woodruff, "*Administration of Angels,*" from an address presented to a General Priesthood Meeting, Provo Tabernacle, Sunday evening, March 3, 1889, reported by Arthur Winter, as cited in ***Collected Discourses Delivered by President Wilford Woodruff, His Two Counselors, The Twelve Apostles, and Others***, comp., ed. Brian H. Stuy, 5 Volumes (Woodland Hills, Utah: B. H. S. Publishing, 1987– 1992), Vol. 1, Sunday, March 3, 1889, brackets added.

At the Sunday general session of a YMMIA conference, convened in June, 1889, President Wilford Woodruff said: "I want to add another thing, because I feel it my duty to say it to the Latter-day Saints. There is a feeling—it was so in the days of Joseph Smith—that he was not the man to lead the Church. Even his bosom friends, men with whom he saw the angels of God, Oliver Cowdery and others, considered him a fallen Prophet and thought they ought to lead the Church. This history is before you and before the world." Then President Woodruff testified: "The same feeling was manifest in the days of Brigham Young when he was called to hold the keys of the Presidency . . . There were other men who thought they should be appointed . . . . But ***the God of heaven manifested to you, and to me, and to all men, who were in Nauvoo, upon whom the mantle had fallen***. Brigham Young took his place, and led the Church and Kingdom of God up to the day of his death." ("*The Keys of the Kingdom,*" from an address presented at the Sunday General Session of the Young Men's Mutual Improvement Association [YMMIA] Conference, in the Tabernacle in Salt Lake City, on Sunday, June 2, 1889, as cited in ***The Contributor***, Vol. 10, No. 11 [September, 1889], pp. 382, 383).

the Spirit of the Lord was poured out upon the Saints, that the mantle of the Prophet did visibly fall upon Brigham Young as a divine and sacred witness, as an assurance, that the keys and authority restored from heaven were not lost but continued, and the Saints were able to associate the office and power of the martyred Joseph, who was gone, with the living Brigham.

Addendum

Following are a few selected testimonies of some who were eyewitness that the mantle of the Prophet Joseph Smith fell upon Brigham Young at the close of the morning meeting at the Stand, Thursday, August 8, 1844. Although they are too lengthy to include in the preceding narrative, they are inserted here for the larger perspective they bring to the account, and for the corroboration and expansion of detail they provide.

In the narrative, except for Presidents of the Church whose names and histories are well known, the testimonies of witnesses were supplemented by brief biographical sketches so that the reader might have some sense of the faith, devotion, and commitment to truth of the witnesses. The following testimonies have likewise been supplemented.

These sketches are not presented as definitive biographical essays about the persons indicated, but are intended only as a glimpse into their lives, and to reassure the reader that these witnesses were not deranged enthusiasts, but men and women, and children, of spirituality, perception, courage and independent mind, familiar with sacrifice and hardship, devoted to the Lord and determined to serve Him. And they represent the broad spectrum of the early Church, children, and parents, prophets, leaders and followers, husbands and wives, artisans, apostles, farmers. Some of them had a few years experience in the faith and some were just barely baptized. Some were veterans of persecution and understood, from the ravages of Missouri, the price required to build the cities of God, while some were just landed by river steamer at Nauvoo expecting to see Zion already raised to her splendor. Some were native to western Illinois and surrounding areas, some were from the principal cities of the young American nation, and some were just arrived from the teeming cities of Great Britain. The sketches are only representative of a great number of others that could be cited, that perhaps, someday, will be cited.

Some of the testimonies were apparently written soon after the Thursday morning meeting at the Stand, for example, the record of Mary Pugh Scott,[94] who wrote that "after the Prophet Joseph's death there was great worry and confusion about who should be the President . . ." Mary accompanied her husband John to the meeting on Thursday, August 8, 1844. "We all bore testimonies of the transfiguration of Brigham Young. While he was speaking he seemed to have the voice of

---

94. Her testimony, that the mantle of the Prophet Joseph Smith fell upon Brigham Young, was noted in her *"Life Story of Mary Pugh [Scott],"* which was written in 1848, following her arrival in Salt Lake City. (Typescript copy, Utah State Historical Society, Salt Lake City, Utah. Also cited in Carol Cornwall Madsen, *"Mary Pugh Scott,"* ***Journey to Zion: Voices from the Mormon Trail*** [Salt Lake City: Deseret Book Company, 1997], pp. 396–403).

the Prophet Joseph Smith. We also saw the form of Joseph Smith before us." She concluded her witness, "there was no doubt in our hearts and minds from then on, as to who should be our leader. The Scott family knew unitedly that Brigham Young was the right man for the right place."[95]

---

95. Mary Pugh Scott was born Saturday, November 10, 1821, at Dilwyn Commons, Leominster, Hereford, England, the twin daughter of Edward Pugh and Mary Bailey. She attended school at Dilwyn Commons, at Earldisland School, and at Haven Dilwyn, a private school. Her conversion to the Church greatly displeased her parents, but she decided to emigrate to America to be with the Saints, reaching Nauvoo in 1842. She married John Scott on Sunday, March 2, 1845. He was "a very prominent man in military affairs in the early days. He held the rank of Colonel in the First Regiment of the Nauvoo Legion. He was also a body guard of the Prophet Joseph Smith, and he was one of his best, loyal, and true friends." The Scotts left Nauvoo in March, 1846, traveled west with the Heber C. Kimball company. Her husband had the care of a party of ten wagons in the train. Mary had a son, Hyrum, just under two years old as they crossed the plains. She was amused at her situation, noting, "here we . . . who have been raised in luxury, are bravely trying to drive a mule team across the plains, holding our babies. We take turns driving. You can just imagine we three women climbing in and out over wagon wheels to cook on the camp fire and wash clothes." The Scotts arrived in the Salt Lake Valley on Sunday, September 24, 1848, the same year that she wrote her history. She died in Salt Lake City on Thursday, January 5, 1905, at the age of 84.

Other early references to the transformation of Brigham Young include a diary entry by George Laub, who wrote, on Wednesday, March 4, 1846: "Now when President Young arose to address the congregation his voice was the voice of Bro[ther] Joseph and his face appeared as Joseph's face, [and] should I have not seen his face but heard his voice I should have declared that it was Joseph." (***Journal of George Laub 1814–1846***, Wednesday, March 4, 1846, Church Historical Department, spelling and grammar adjusted and brackets added).

George Laub was born Wednesday, October 5, 1814, in Earl Township, Lancaster, Pennsylvania. His father died when he was eight years old and his mother surrendered him to George Weydler, a well-to-do farmer and businessman, who adopted him. He learned the carpenter's trade. He heard Erastus Snow and others preach and was baptized on March 12, 1842. He served a mission in Pennsylvania before joining the Saints in Nauvoo in 1843. He worked on the Nauvoo Temple and was present at the meeting at the Stand. After leaving Nauvoo with the main body of the Saints, he remained at Winter Quarters for

Others made a record of the events of that day in 1844 or 1845.[96] But other testimonies, for example, the testimony of Wilford Woodruff, recorded as President Woodruff followed up a sermon presented by Elder B. H. Roberts, in the Assembly Hall, by adding his own witness, are recollections over long years. Wilford Woodruff, just one week short of his 85th birthday and 48 years after the meeting at the Stand, said:

> *"Before [the Prophet] died he organized the Church with Apostles . . . and the whole government of the Church . . . and*

---

a period of several years building houses to assist other emigrants, but finally traveled to Utah in 1852. He married Anna Elizabeth Ericksen, a convert and immigrant from Alborg, Denmark, on Tuesday, March 11, 1856 in the Endowment House. (She died in St. George, Washington County, Utah, in 1926 at the age of 87). He built his own home in Salt Lake City following his marriage, but left it to accept a call to assist in the settlement of southern Utah in 1863. He labored as a joiner or carpenter building houses, mills, the Salt Lake Theater and other public buildings including the St. George Temple, and served as foreman in the construction of the St. George tabernacle. He died on Sunday, November 14, 1880, at St. George, at the age of 76.

96. There were other early references to events of Thursday, August 8, 1844. One year before George Laub recorded his experience at the Stand, in 1845, William Burton wrote that "the spirit of Joseph appeared to rest upon Brigham." (***Journal of William Burton***, May, 1845, Church Historical Department). Subsequent to the revelation of Sunday, July 8, 1838 (D&C 118:4–5), by which the Lord commanded that the Twelve should take leave of the Church and start for their mission to England from the Temple lot at Far West, the Saints had been driven from Missouri and enemies of the Church gloated that the Twelve would never return to Far West to commence their mission to England from the Temple lot. William Burton was one of the faithful party who, despite threats from the enemies of the Church, assembled at the Temple site at Far West, Missouri, in the early morning of Friday, April 26, 1839, to fulfill that revelation. He served as clerk of the 15th Semi-annual General Conference, in Nauvoo, in October, 1845. Not long after arrival of the Saints in the Salt Lake Valley, William Burton was called on the mission to the British Isles and he died in March, 1851, at Edinburgh, Scotland, while serving as a missionary.

that Priesthood . . . remained with the people after his death . . . I am a living witness to the testimony that Joseph gave to the Twelve Apostles when all of us received our endowments under his hands. I remember the last speech that he ever gave us before his death. It was before we started upon our mission to the East. He stood upon his feet some three hours. The room was filled as with consuming fire, his face was as clear as amber, and he was clothed upon by the power of God. He laid before us our duty. He laid before us the fullness of this great work of God; and in his remarks to us he said: 'I have had sealed upon my head every key, every power, every principle of life and salvation that God has ever given to any man who ever lived upon the face of the earth. And these principles and this Priesthood and power belong to this great and last dispensation which the God of heaven has set His hand to establish in the earth. Now,' said he, addressing the Twelve, 'I have sealed upon your heads every key, every power, and every principle which the Lord has sealed

---

Still earlier, on Friday, November 15, 1844, Henry and Catherine Brooke addressed a letter from Nauvoo to Leonard and Mary Pickel in New York stating that Brigham Young "favours Br[other] Joseph, both in person, and manner of speaking more than any person ever you saw, looks like another." (Henry and Catherine Brooke to Leonard and Mary Pickel, dated Friday, November 15, 1844, Leonard Pickel Papers, Frederick W. and Carrie S. Beinecke Library of Western Americana, Yale University, New Haven, Connecticut, brackets added).

And about the same time as the Brooke statement, on Wednesday, November 20, 1844, Arza Hinckley recorded that "Brigham Young, on whom the mantle of the Prophet Joseph has fallen, is a man of God and keeps all things in good order." (***The Journal of Arza Hinckley***, Wednesday, November 20, 1844, L. Tom Perry Special Collections, Harold B. Lee Library, Brigham Young University, Provo, Utah). Arza Erastus Hinckley was born on Wednesday, August 15, 1827, in Leeds County, Ontario, Canada, a son of Nathaniel Hinckley and Lois Judd. He was baptized in 1838 en route to Missouri where he joined the flight of the Saints from northern Missouri to Nauvoo. At Nauvoo, he labored on the Nauvoo Temple.

upon my head' . . . After addressing us in this manner he said: 'I tell you, the burden of this kingdom now rests upon your shoulders; you have got to bear it off in all the world, and if you don't do it you will be damned' . . . After that hour we departed for our mission, not knowing anything of this terrible tragedy until we received an account of their death some time afterwards . . . [As soon as was possible, after hearing of the Martyrdom,] we returned to Nauvoo. It has been repeated to you here tonight what was done at that conference in Nauvoo. I do not know whether there is any one present here tonight but myself who was there at the conference—there are but few living who were present on that occasion. Brigham stepped forth as a leader of Israel . . . and when Brigham Young arose and commenced speaking, as has been said, if my eyes had not been so I could see, if I had not seen him with my own eyes, there is no one that could have convinced me that it was not Joseph Smith speaking. It was as the voice and face of Joseph Smith; and any one can testify to this who was acquainted with these two men."[97]

Following the exodus of the Saints from Nauvoo, in Iowa, he joined the Mormon Battalion. He spent the winter of 1846 with the "sick" detachment of the Battalion at Pueblo, Colorado, and traveled with that group to the Salt Lake Valley, arriving on Thursday, July 29, 1847, only five days after the Pioneer Company. He lived in Salt Lake City until 1864, and was then assigned to assist with settlement of Summit County, where he served as probate judge and assisted with construction of the Union Pacific Railroad. In 1882, he was called to serve a mission to Arizona. At the end of his mission in 1884, he relocated to Rexburg, Bingham County, Idaho, where he served as a Patriarch from 1887 until his death on Monday, February 18, 1901, at the age of 74. (See Jenson, "*Arza Erastus Hinckley*," ***LDS Biographical Encyclopedia***, Vol. 4, p. 746).

97. Elder B. H. Roberts, at the time one of the First Seven Presidents of the Seventy, presented a major address entitled "*The Priesthood and the Right of Succession*" at a meeting of the Young Men's Mutual Improvement Association of

But each of these noble souls were not only witnesses to these events by their words, but by their very lives, by their departure, soon after the events in question, on an overland trek of over eleven hundred miles, leaving behind their homes, businesses and farms, places of manufacture, and the relative comforts of an established community; leaving behind them the great temple which had become the center of their hopes and dreams, taking with them their courage and their hopes, and only what possessions they could stuff into wagons, load onto horses, or carry on their backs.

If they themselves did not have family members who were torn away to serve in the Mormon Battalion, they assisted on the trail and sought to encourage others who did. If they did not go into the world to preach the Gospel while their wives and families and loved ones pressed westward into a "waste howling wilderness"[98] without their companionship and their help, they marched by the side of others who did. And if they

---

the Salt Lake Stake, that convened in the Assembly Hall on Temple Square, on Tuesday evening, February 23, 1892. President Wilford Woodruff attended the meeting. In the course of his remarks, Elder Roberts recalled the events of the "prayer meeting" at the Stand in Nauvoo, on Thursday, August 8, 1844, described the mantle of the Prophet Joseph Smith falling upon Brigham Young, and cited the testimonies of George Q. Cannon and William Carter Staines who were present and witness to the event. He then suggested that perhaps, because so many young people were present, President Woodruff might consider sharing his testimony of the authority that passed from Joseph Smith to Brigham Young. President Woodruff indicated that, at the close of Elder Robert's remarks, he would do so. When Elder Roberts completed his address and sat down, President Wilford Woodruff arose and addressed the congregation. ("*'Remarks' delivered by President Wilford Woodruff at the conclusion of Elder Roberts' discourse,*" ***Collected Discourses***, Vol. 2, Tuesday, February 23, 1892, brackets added).

98. Deuteronomy 32:10. Compare President Orson Hyde, "*Common Salvation,*" from an address presented in the Old Tabernacle in Great Salt Lake City, Friday, September 23, 1853, as cited in ***Journal of Discourses***, Vol. 2, p. 119.

did not perish themselves on this trek to the Great Basin, they buried along the way others who did.

This is not the stuff of hollow testimonials. This is not the substance of perjured witnesses. This is the course of honest men and women, who knew that the keys and authorities with all of the attendant blessings, precious and dear to them, that had been conferred upon the Prophet Joseph Smith by holy angels, had not been swept away by the Martyrdom, but remained in the earth, and continued with Brigham Young and his associates in the Twelve, and would never be taken away.

Testimony of William Adams

William Adams,[99] a convert to the Church from Ireland who arrived in Nauvoo shortly before the Martyrdom in 1844, wrote that

> *"Joseph had sent letters to the Twelve to hurry home to Nauvoo, and among the first [to arrive] was Sidney Rigdon who hurried home from Pittsburgh and laid claim to be guardian . . . and was using his influence to get the Saints to sustain him. He began to organize the Church, ordaining apostles, and preached to the Saints sustaining his claims . . .*

99. William Adams's record is from his *"Autobiography 1822–1849,"* January, 1894, Typescript, L. Tom Perry Special Collections, Harold B. Lee Library, Brigham Young University, pp. 12–14, brackets added. Williams Adams was born Tuesday, January 8, 1822, in prosperous circumstances, in Hillsborough County, Ireland, the second son in a family of eight children, five boys and three girls. He was baptized in 1842, at the age of twenty, and raised a branch of the Church in Crawford Burn, Ireland. Two years later, he emigrated with his wife and son,

and appointed a day for a general meeting for the Saints to sustain him. His object was to [be] sustained before the brethren of the Twelve would arrive in Nauvoo. Brother Parley P. Pratt was among the first to arrive, and he and Brother Willard Richards, two of the Twelve, labored with Sidney not be in a hurry until the Twelve would arrive, but he was determined to have the vote taken according to his appointment. Brigham Young and Heber C. Kimball arrived one day before the meeting, and others had arrived previously so that nearly all the Twelve were in Nauvoo. William Marks, president of the stake, called the meeting to order, and took charge of the meeting. After the opening exercises Rigdon spoke of his claim as guardian . . . showing the necessity of the office, which took between one half to one hour.

"There was a great multitude attending the meeting; more than one half the crowd could not find seats, and stood on their feet. Never were so many at one meeting that I ever saw. I was sitting down and could not see the speakers on the

---

embarking from Liverpool on the "*Fanny*" to New Orleans, and from New Orleans on the "*Maid of Iowa,*" hoping to reach Nauvoo in time for the April 1844 General Conference. They encountered much hardship along the way, including attacks by mobs at various stops along the Mississippi—(at one dock hostile citizens rushed on board and succeeded in setting the "*Maid of Iowa*" on fire; the fire was extinguished and the boat suffered no structural damage), but they were disappointed to arrive in Nauvoo just after the April General Conference. He did attend the meeting at the Stand on Thursday, August 8, 1844. He labored as a stonecutter on the Nauvoo Temple, received his Temple blessings there with his wife, and following the exodus from Nauvoo, continued as a stonecutter in Illinois and Missouri, including work on the state house in Springfield. By early 1849, when he had saved enough to acquire an outfit to make the trek west to Utah, he joined with a few other families and traveled west to join the body of the Church in Utah. The family settled in Parowan, in southern Utah, and eventually relocated to Bluff, San Juan County, in southeastern Utah, where he died Monday, September 30, 1901.

Stand. I was listening very attentively, so that I could hear every word.

"I heard a voice speaking; I was surprised, and jumping to my feet, expecting Joseph the Prophet was speaking, having heard him often in public and private, so that I was quite acquainted with his voice. This was a strong testimony that the Twelve Apostles were the rightful leaders of the Church and that the mouth of Joseph had fallen on Brigham Young."

Testimony of George Laub

George Laub,[100] a pioneer diarist who recorded accounts of some of the Prophet Joseph's Nauvoo sermons, and a skilled carpenter who assisted with construction of the Nauvoo Temple, the St. George Temple, the St. George Tabernacle, other public buildings and private homes, testified:

"Sidney Rigdon having [had] a mission appointed him by [the Prophet] Joseph to Pittsburgh before his death [prior to the martyrdom]. Now after his death [after the martyrdom], Sidney came in all the haste in him to Nauvoo from Pittsburgh to claim the presidency of the Church, him not knowing that Joseph sent him out of the way to get rid of him. Now when he returned to Nauvoo he called all the people

100. George Laub's testimony is recorded in the ***Journal of George Laub 1814–1846***, Wednesday, March 4, 1846, Church Historical Department. This is the smallest of four personal journals that he kept faithfully throughout the course of his life. The other three—large, comprehensive journals—reflect the detail of his life until his death in St. George at the age of 76. Spelling and grammar has been adjusted and brackets added. See footnote #95 above).

together to choose [for] them a guardian, as he expressed [or described] himself. Now, said he, 'the Church is fourteen years old and it is the duty of the Church to choose a guardian.' [He] preached there for two days on that subject . . . Just about the time that the vote was to be taken for him to be president and guardian . . . the Lord would have the Twelve to come home and I felt to praise God to see Bro[ther] Brigham Young walk upon the Stand then. These positive revelations of Rigdon's were only guess so, and he thinks so, and hope so, while the Lord [had] told him how to proceed before according to his own mouth[101] *and afterwards only supposed them so [Sidney did not properly regard previous revelations].*

"Now when President Young arose to address the congregation his voice was the voice of Bro[ther] Joseph and his face appeared as Joseph's face, and should I have not seen his face but [only] heard his voice, I should have declared that it was Joseph. Now he [Brigham Young] arose and commenced speaking, saying 'I would rather have mourned forty days than to come here, and if Rigdon was the legal heir to lead the Church, why did he not stop to [wait at or remain in] Pittsburgh till we came and accompanied him as I had wr[itten] to him? But he was afraid that he could not carry out his designs and conspiracy underhanded, etc.' Immediately Rigdon's followers armed them[selves] with the weapons of death and with the brandy jug so that they might have the spirits of their calling, for Rigdon was filled with that same brandy spirit. [Since William] Marks[102] *was his first council [his primary advisor], and the party having been*

101. See D&C 100:9–11; 124:103–110.
102. See footnote #38 above.

counseled by Rigdon to go and kill the first man that would say aught against him[,] . . . Marks told him and them if they did they would all be killed for their recompense [they would be brought to justice], and so they remained quiet."

Testimony of Rachel Ridgeway Ivins Grant

Rachel Ridgeway Ivins Grant,[103] the wife of Jedediah M. Grant who was Second Counselor to President Brigham Young, and mother of President Heber J. Grant, testified that

". . . after the Prophet's death when Sidney Rigdon came to Nauvoo and spoke, he thought that it was his right and

---

103. Rachel Ridgeway Ivins Grant's witness was published in *"Joseph Smith," **The Young Women's Journal**,* Vol. 16 (1905), p. 551. Rachel Ivins Grant was born in New Jersey in 1821, the daughter of Caleb Ivins and Edith Ridgeway Ivins—her father was a prosperous merchant and her parents were both devout Dutch Quakers. In 1837, she attended a Mormon meeting in Hornerstown, New Jersey, where she listened to the Prophet Joseph Smith and Elder Erastus Snow. She visited Nauvoo in 1842, remaining until 1844, and became acquainted with the Prophet's family and to some extent with the Prophet himself during that period. She was quite young when she visited Nauvoo, and was not then a member of the church, but she became convinced of the truth of the work, joined the Church just before she turned twenty, partly through the preaching of her future husband, and ever after remained true to her testimony of the divinity of the mission of the Prophet Joseph. She was in Nauvoo in the Summer of 1844, and was present to witness the divine manifestation which the Lord provided to the Saints at the close of the "prayer meeting" that had been convened on Thursday, August 8, 1844, at the Stand. Later, she accompanied the body of the Church to the Valley of the Great Salt Lake where she married in 1855, becoming the seventh wife in plural marriage to Jedediah Morgan Grant, Second Counselor to President Brigham Young and the first Mayor of Salt Lake City. When her husband died just nine days after their first child was born, in 1856, she moved from the substantial Grant home to a modest cottage and refused to accept assistance from

privilege to be President of the Church. [But] President Young jumped right up on the S[tand] and spoke. If you had had your eyes shut, you would have thought it was the Prophet. In fact he looked like him, his very countenance seemed to change, and he spoke like him."

Testimony of Henry Shuler Buckwalter

Henry Shuler Buckwalter,[104] who was a native of Pennsylvania, who traveled with his widowed mother and five siblings to Nauvoo in 1842 and was baptized in the Mississippi River in 1843 at the age of 13, recalled that as a young man

"I witnessed the trying scenes surrounding the martyrdom of the Prophet and Patriarch. I was at the meeting

---

the Church, but insisted on supporting herself and her son by taking in washing, custom sewing, and taking in boarders. Her son was Heber J. Grant who became successor to the Prophet Joseph Smith as the seventh President of the Church. Rachel Grant died in Salt Lake City in 1894 at the age of 73.

104. Henry Shuler Buckwalter was born in Chester County, Pennsylvania on Thursday, May 12, 1831, the son of John Buckwalter and Sarah Shuler. His parents joined the Church in 1839 but his father died in 1841 before the family could gather with the Saints. Henry traveled with his widowed mother and five siblings to Nauvoo, was baptized in the Mississippi River in July, 1843, and attended the meeting at the Stand on Thursday, August 8, 1844, at the age of 13. He left Nauvoo with the Saints in 1846, stayed in Iowa one year, and then traveled to St. Louis in 1848 where he remained until April, 1852, then journeyed to the Salt Lake Valley, arriving on Wednesday, August 11 that same year. He settled in the Salt Lake City 9th Ward. It is unclear what became of his mother, but two sisters, Margaret and Elizabeth, and one brother, John Edwin, came to Utah. At the call of President Brigham Young, he traveled east with a company of missionaries, led by Elder John Taylor, who ordained him an elder. He served for two years, 1855 and 1856.

called by Sidney Rigdon Aug[ust] 8, 1844, when he proclaimed himself a guardian to the Church. I saw and heard Brigham Young when his voice and manner became changed, so that he talked and looked just like the Prophet Joseph Smith. Together with the body of the Church, I endured the persecutions, which culminated in our expulsion from Nauvoo, by a mob in 1846."

Testimony of Ezra Taft Benson

Ezra Taft Benson,[105] who served as a member of the Twelve from 1846 to 1869, and is the grandfather of President Ezra Taft Benson, recorded that

". . . the news came out that our Prophet was martyred in Carthage Jail [and] we found our mission was at the end. The question arose by [Brother John] Pack, 'Who will now lead

---

He served in Echo Canyon during the campaign of resistance against Johnston's Army in 1857, and then on the eastern plains as part of an expedition to protect the overland mail from Indian attacks, to assist in locating a new colony in the Black Hills, near Ft. Laramie, and as a teamster to bring emigrants from the Missouri River to the Salt Lake Valley. He married Harriet Victoria Orton on Tuesday, September 24, 1861; they were the parents of nine children, and resided in American Fork, in Utah County, until 1877. The Buckwalters then returned to Salt Lake City, where he died in 1908 at the age of 77. (See Jenson, *"Henry Shuler Buckwalkter," **LDS Biographical Encyclopedia***, Vol. 1, p.604).

105. Ezra Taft Benson's testimony was published as a part of his *"Autobiography,"* in ***The Juvenile Instructor***, Vol. 80 (1945), pp. 213–214, brackets added. Ezra Taft Benson was born in Mendon, Massachusetts in 1811. He worked as a farmer and hotel keeper, married, and eventually obeyed impressions to travel to the West, travels which ultimately brought him to Nauvoo in 1839 where he became acquainted with the Church and was baptized in 1840. He departed on a

the Church?' I told him I did not know, but I knew who would lead me and that would be the Twelve Apostles . . . [This] was a time of great distress and grief on account of Joseph Smith's death . . . I found Sidney Rigdon contending for the right to lead the Church and in a few days the Twelve Apostles arrived, and when Bro. Brigham Young rose before the people and spoke, it was very easy to see who possessed the mantle of Joseph Smith. Truly, as Jesus said, my sheep hear my voice, but a stranger they will not follow, for many said when they heard Brigham talk, truly it was not Brigham, but the voice of Joseph."

---

mission to the Eastern States in 1842, served until late 1843, then returned to Nauvoo and remained there through the April Conference of 1844, and then departed for a second mission to the Eastern States. After learning of the Martyrdom, he returned to Nauvoo and was present at the "prayer meeting" convened at the Stand on Thursday, August 8, 1844. Subsequently, he served as a member of the Nauvoo Stake High Council, served another mission to Boston, and then returned to rejoin the main body of the Saints in Iowa where he was called to the Quorum of the Twelve. He traveled with the pioneer company to the Salt Lake Valley and then returned that same year to Winter Quarters where he was appointed to preside, with Orson Hyde and George A. Smith, at Pottawatamie, Iowa. He returned to the Salt Lake Valley in 1849, served as a member of the provisional government of the State of Deseret and, after organization of the Territory of Utah, served several terms as a member of the territorial legislature. As an Apostle, Ezra Taft Benson served a number of missions, including an assignment to preside over the British Mission, and a mission to Hawaii with Lorenzo Snow. He also served missions in Utah. In 1860, just after he had completed construction of a lovely new house on Main Street in Salt Lake City near the Temple block, he was asked to sell the home and assigned to preside over the Mormon settlements in Cache Valley. He responded without hesitation. In 1869, he contracted to provide grade for a section of the Central Pacific Railroad, but the railroad failed to settle the contract satisfactorily. Soon after, he died suddenly in Ogden, Weber County, Utah, on Friday, September 3, 1869 at the age of 58. He was the grandfather of Ezra Taft Benson, who succeeded the Prophet Joseph Smith as the thirteenth President of the Church.

Testimony of George Morris

George Morris,[106] a convert from England, who labored diligently on the Nauvoo Temple and received his blessings there before making the journey to Utah, recalled:

> *"[In the month of] August of 1844, a special meeting was appointed for the Church to come together to hear what he [Sidney Rigdon] had to say on the subject [of who should lead the Church]. He did not occupy the Stand where Brigham and some of the rest of the Twelve were, but he stood in a*

---

106. George Morris's record is taken from his "*Autobiography,*" Typescript, L. Tom Perry Special Collections, Harold B. Lee Library, Brigham Young University, p. 26, brackets added. George Morris was born in Hanley, Cheshire, England August 23,1816, and was christened on Thursday, September 26, 1816, in Bunbury, Cheshire, England, the eldest of six children reared in a strict Methodist home. He worked at odd jobs as a youth, as a hired hand on farms, as a livery attendant, and at one time in a steam boiler plant where, due to the noise, he suffered permanent hearing loss. He married Jane Higgenbotham at Parrish Church, Ashton, Cheshire, England, on Monday, January 6, 1840. She gave birth to a daughter in January, 1841, but died the following April; the child lingered until October and then died also. That same year he joined the Church, emigrated to Nauvoo the next year, and on Wednesday, August 23, 1843, at the age of 26 years, married again, Hannah Maria Newberry, also a convert, from Strongville, Cuyahoga, Ohio, at Nauvoo. After the Martyrdom, he assisted with construction of the Nauvoo Temple, and after he and his wife had received their Temple blessings, they made the journey to the Valley of the Great Salt Lake, arriving in 1848. They were the parents of twelve children. When he entered into the order of plural marriage, he became estranged from his first wife who charged that he was not equitable but showed partiality among the various families. When he was arrested under authority of the Edmunds bill, he was acquitted by the testimony of his first wife and their eldest daughter's testimony that he had not lived with that family for a number of years. In Utah he worked initially as a well digger, and later at many other jobs, but principally as a stone mason. Later, he moved to St. George to assist with the construction of the St. George Temple. Following dedication of the Temple, he returned to Salt Lake City where he died on Friday, January 29, 1897 at the age of 80.

wagon with some of his supporters in another part of the congregation . . . and ordinarily was [a] very eloquent and pleasing speaker but at that time he made a very feeble effort.

"[When] President Young . . . arose to speak, I was sitting holding down my head reflecting upon what had been said by [Sidney] Rigdon when I was startled by hearing Joseph's voice. He [Joseph Smith] had a way of clearing his throat before he began to speak by a peculiar effort of his own, like Ah Hem, but it had a different sound from him [compared] to anyone else. I raised my head suddenly and the first thing I saw was Joseph as plain as I ever saw him in my life. He was dressed in a light linen suit with a light leghorn hat such as he used to wear in the warm weather and the first words he said were, 'Right here [is] the authority to lead this Church,' at the same time striking his hand on his bosom, and he went on to utter several sentences in Joseph's voice as clear and distinct as I ever heard Joseph speak, and his gestures and appearance were perfect. This was testimony sufficient for me where the authority rested."

Testimony of William Bryan Pace

William Bryan Pace,[107] a native of Tennessee who relocated to Nauvoo with his parents, was baptized in Nauvoo, was present at the meeting at the Stand, Thursday, August 8, 1844 at the age of twelve, and who, when not yet fifteen years old, marched with the Mormon Battalion" into California, recorded:

107. William Bryan Pace's testimony is from in his *"Autobiography,"* Typescript, L. Tom Perry Special Collections, Harold B. Lee Library, Brigham Young University, p. 7, brackets added. William Pace was born on Wednesday,

"... next ... was the arrival of Sidney Rigdon, Brigham Young and the twelve who were absent at the Prophet's death, and the struggle that followed.

"[At the Stand,] Sidney Rigdon spent what seemed to me several hours, haranguing the people on the importance of making him their leader, after which, Brigham arose and said only a word, when it was observed by the whole congregation that the mantle of 'Joseph' was upon him, in word, gesture and general appearance.

"The people arose en masse to their feet astonished, as it appeared that Joseph had returned and was speaking to the people. I was small and got upon a bench that I might more fully witness the 'phenomena.' There was no longer any question as to who was the leader ..."

February 9, 1832 in Double Springs, Rutherford, Tennessee. His parents, James Pace and Lucinda Gibson Strickland Pace, relocated the family to Shelby County, Illinois, and, after joining the Church in 1838, relocated to Nauvoo. His father was a farmer and pursued that vocation throughout his life, except when, in the Nauvoo period, he served as a bodyguard for the Prophet and later for Brigham Young, and also when he served with the Mormon Battalion. William was baptized in Nauvoo at the age of eight, and was twelve at the time of the Martyrdom and the events which are the subject of this study. At fourteen, his parents crossed into Iowa and journeyed to Council Bluffs. There his father enlisted and was made a First Lieutenant in the 'Mormon Battalion.' As an officer, his father was entitled to an aide and William Bryan was chosen. Thus, although only a boy, he made the trek with the Battalion to San Diego and his history is one of the primary accounts of that march. While the Battalion was bivouacked at San Louis Rey, William borrowed the muskets from soldiers who were ill and joined in the daily morning and afternoon drills. When the Battalion was mustered out, on Thursday, July 1, 1847, he marched in the company commanded by his father, James Pace, back to join the main body of the Church. By this means, he learned military maneuvers and tactics. In later life, he served as a general defending against the threat of Johnston's army. He also served with distinction in the Indian wars, and served a number of terms in the territorial legislature. He died at Orem, Utah County, Utah, on Friday, June 7, 1907 at the age of 75.

Testimony of Homer Duncan

Homer Duncan[108] was a native of Vermont. He joined the Church in 1838, subsequently served several missions, and became a cattle rancher in Utah. A man with deep sensitivities to the Spirit, he received frequent ministrations in visions and dreams. He recalled:

> *"At the special meeting held at Nauvoo after Joseph Smith's death—at the time that the mantle of the Prophet of the Lord fell upon Brigham Young—I sat listening to someone speaking, with my head down, my face hid in the palms of my hands and my elbows resting on my knees. While in this position Brigham Young came to the stand and commenced to speak with the voice of Joseph the Prophet. Being so well acquainted with the Prophet's voice, I nearly sprang from my seat, through astonishment; but I sat and heard the Prophet Joseph's voice as long as Brigham Young was speaking. Not only did the voice of Brigham sound like that of Joseph, but the*

---

108. Homer Duncan's testimony is preserved in Jenson, *"Homer Duncan,"* ***The LDS Biographical Encyclopedia***, Vol. 1, p. 622. Homer Duncan was born Sunday, January 19, 1815, at Barnet, Vermont, a son of John Duncan and Betsy Taylor Putnam, a great grandson of General Israel Putnam who served under General Washington in the Revolutionary War. He was deeply religious, and was favored with visions. He was baptized in the Grand river, Adam-Ondi-Ahman, Missouri, in 1838, and the following year, at Far West, was ordained a Seventy by Heber C. Kimball and Amasa Lyman—he would serve as a Seventy for 67 years. He then served a mission to New York and Ontario for two years, his efforts blessed by converts, visions and miraculous healings. He married Asenath Melvina Banker in 1841, and journeyed with her to Nauvoo in 1843. He was present in the meeting at the Stand, Thursday, August 8, 1844. He left Nauvoo with the Saints in 1846, remained at Council Bluffs, Iowa for two years due to illness, and then traveled to the Salt Lake Valley, arriving Monday, October 16, 1848. He

very gestures of his right hand, when he was saying anything very positive, reminded me of Joseph. My decision was then made as to who should lead the Church; for surely the mantle of Joseph had fallen upon Brigham."

Testimony of Robert T. Burton

Robert T. Burton,[109] who was born in Canada in 1821, who served as a Colonel in the Nauvoo Legion and as a Counselor in the Presiding Bishopric for over thirty years, was present at

---

was a successful cattle rancher, settled with his family in the Cottonwoods until 1850, then in Salt Lake City until 1855, served a mission to Texas and led a company of immigrants and 1,300 head of cattle back to the Valley, tended his herds in Rush Valley until 1860, and then served a mission to England. He returned in 1861 with a company of immigrants, and brought another company from Florence, Nebraska the following year. He devoted many years to managing cattle in Cedar City and later in Salt Lake City. There he resided in the Salt Lake City 11th Ward and served as the senior President of the 3rd Quorum of the Seventy until his death on Friday, March 23, 1906, at the age of 91.

109. President Joseph F. Smith, son of Hyrum Smith and nephew of the Prophet Joseph Smith, later fifth in succession to the Prophet as the sixth President of the Church, but at the time Second Counselor in the First Presidency to President Wilford Woodruff, was concerned that insufficient notice was made in the Church of the Prophet Joseph's birthday—December 23. On that day in 1894, a Sunday evening, fifty years after the Martyrdom, he convened a special "Memorial Services in Honor of the Prophet Joseph Smith's Birthday", at the Salt Lake 16th Ward Meeting House. Special guests at these services were those who had personally known the Prophet—there were 23 present, seventeen men and six women; those who had seen the Prophet but had not known him personally—five: four women and one man; those who had been baptized by the Prophet—two: one woman and one man; and those who had been ordained to offices in the Priesthood by the Prophet—there was one man.

In the course of this extraordinary meeting, President Joseph F. Smith presented an address entitled *"Recollections of the Prophet Joseph Smith."* Those who had known the Prophet Joseph were also invited to share their experiences and a

the Stand on Thursday, August 8, 1844, at the age of 23, and later testified:

> *"[I] was on guard in the city of Nauvoo at the time the martyrdom of the Prophets occurred, and well [remember] the conditions, and scenes of those times. [P]rior to that time, and as far as [I] knew, the Latter-day Saints thought it was not possible to take the life of Joseph, the Prophet of God. He had many, many times been arrested, held in custody, and tried, but always acquitted of any charge brought against him. His life was often in imminent peril, but invariably something intervened to preserve his life until the people began to think the wicked could not destroy the life of that great man; and when the awful news came, nobody can tell or feel as those felt who had their lives wound up in that man, the degree of gloom and sadness that pervaded every person in the city of Nauvoo. A large number of the people were in the militia over whom Joseph Smith had been the superior officer. They felt as if they*

---

number of them responded; Bishop Robert T. Burton was one of these. (See *"Recollections of the Prophet Joseph Smith,"* cited in ***Collected Discourses***, Vol. 5, Sunday, December 23, 1894, brackets added).

Bishop Robert T. Burton was born on Thursday, October 25, 1821, in Amherstburg, Ontario, Canada, the tenth of fourteen children of Samuel Burton and Hannah Shipley, immigrants from England. He first learned of the Church in 1837, then lived with his widowed sister in Ohio before returning to Canada where he was baptized in 1838. He journeyed with his father's family toward Far West, but upon learning of the expulsion of the Saints from Missouri, they settled in Walnut Grove, Illinois, where they resided for two years before moving to Nauvoo. He served a mission in 1843 and 1844 in the surrounding states and returned to Nauvoo just prior to the martyrdom. He joined the Nauvoo Brass Band, the choir, and the cavalry of the Nauvoo Legion and was posted to guard duty through the difficult Summer of 1844. He was present at the Stand on Thursday, August 8, 1844. He served a mission to the surrounding counties of Illinois in 1845. He married Maria Susan Haven Thursday, December 18, 1845,

must go right to Carthage, and from there follow the fiends that had destroyed the life of the Prophet. But this was overcome. In time it became the question who was going to lead the people. One said, 'follow me,' and another, 'follow me,' until some of the people became confused. Most of the Apostles and leading Elders were absent on missions. I was well acquainted with the Prophet. I was imperfectly acquainted with Brigham Young. When Brigham Young returned, and arose in the congregation and began to speak, I arose from my seat, as did hundreds of others, to look at Joseph. His voice, his language, every expression seemed to come from Joseph himself. It was a testimony to many hundreds of the Latter-day Saints that from that time to the present has never left their memories for

---

and together they left Nauvoo, crossing the Mississippi on the ice on Wednesday, February 11, 1846. They cared for his aged parents and remained in Iowa until 1848, then journeyed to the Salt Lake Valley, where they settled in Salt Lake City. He served in the cavalry of the territorial militia, eventually advancing to the rank of major-general, defending settlers from Indian attack, in Utah County, Box Elder County, Tooele County and Wyoming. He also served as part of a "corps of observation" dispatched from Salt Lake City to assess movements of the Federal army's approach to Utah in 1857, as Salt Lake City constable, United States deputy marshal, sheriff, assessor and tax collector, as a member of the Salt Lake City council for 17 years, as a member of the territorial legislative council for 32 years, on a committee of three including Abraham O. Smoot and Silas S. Smith to compile, arrange and publish the laws of Utah Territory; and for four years, 1880 to 1884, as a regent of the University of Deseret. He served in the Bishopric and as Bishop of the Salt Lake 15th Ward from 1859 to 1869, as a missionary to the eastern States and as an aide to William H. Hooper, Utah's delegate to Congress until 1873, and then as a missionary to England and Europe until 1875. While in Europe, in 1874, he was appointed Second Counselor to Presiding Bishop Edward Hunter, and in 1884, as First Counselor to Presiding Bishop William B. Preston—he would serve in the Presiding Bishopric for over 33 years until his death in Salt Lake City, Monday, November 11, 1907, at the age of 86. (See Jenson, *"Robert Taylor Burton,"* ***LDS Biographical Encyclopedia,*** Vol. 1, pp. 238–241).

a moment. By it God communicated to His people who the successor of Joseph was. It has been a great comfort to me. **I speak it here in all soberness and thoughtfulness that I rose to my feet to look upon Joseph Smith because I thought I heard his voice, and felt his spirit and the influence that he had.**"[110]

Testimony of Bathsheba W. Smith

Bathsheba W. Smith,[111] who was a native of West Virginia, the wife of Elder George Albert Smith who was a member of the Quorum of the Twelve Apostles, his widow for 34 years,

---

110. Others arose in that same meeting to speak of the mantle of the Prophet Joseph resting upon Brigham Young. Edward Rushton, who was acquainted with the Prophet in Nauvoo, was present at the Stand on Thursday, August 8, 1844, who journeyed to the Salt Lake Valley and was one of the first settlers in the Hunter area, and who died in Salt Lake City on Wednesday, December 28, 1904, stated that he "became acquainted with the Prophet" on Wednesday, April 13, 1842, when he "landed at Nauvoo as an emigrant," and bore testimony, "similar to Bishop Burton, of Joseph's appearance being manifest in Brigham Young." Oliver G. Workman, who was born Sunday, January 7, 1827, in Tennessee, who joined the Church and moved to Nauvoo where he was present at the Stand on Thursday, August 8, 1844, who served as a member of the Mormon Battalion, and who died in Salt Lake City, Monday, July 28, 1902, also stood in the meeting and said he "was an eye-witness of many of the transactions related this evening," that he "was also present when the mantle of Joseph fell upon Brigham Young" and that he wished to join "his testimony with those previously given as to the miraculous manifestation." (See "*Recollections of the Prophet,*" as cited in ***Collected Discourses***, Vol. 5, Sunday, December 23, 1894, emphasis added).

111. Bathsheba W. Smith was one of six women who had personally known the Prophet Joseph Smith, who was present at the special "Memorial Services in Honor of the Prophet Joseph Smith's Birthday," at the Salt Lake 16th Ward Meeting House, as cited in footnote #109 above, and also in "*Recollections of a Prophet,*" ***Collected Discourses***, Vol. 5, Sunday, December 23, 1894.

and who served as the fourth General President of the Relief Society, testified:

> *"I rise to say that I know Joseph Smith was a true Prophet of God. I know that God, through that Prophet, revealed the endowments. I received mine in company with my husband when Joseph was living. I never had anything to disturb my faith. I know that President Young was the lawful successor of*

Bathsheba Wilson Smith was born on Friday, May 3, 1822, in Shinnsten, Harrison County, West Virginia, the daughter of Mark Bigler and Susannah Ogden. In her youth she was an accomplished horseback rider. She was baptized Monday, August 21, 1837, at the age of 15; most of her family joined at the same time, and they journeyed to join the main body of the Church at Far West, Missouri. They arrived just at the time of the Haun's Mill atrocities, personally witnessed the death of David W. Patten, President of the Quorum of the Twelve, and the incarceration of the Prophet and others, journeyed with the Saints to Quincey, Illinois, welcomed the Prophet there in 1840, and moved with the Saints to Nauvoo. On Sunday, July 25, 1841, she was married to George A. Smith, junior member of the Twelve. In 1843, they received their endowments and were sealed, and were then privileged to attend special meetings in a room above the Prophet's store where she heard the Prophet teach the Twelve, confer upon them all the keys and powers and authorities which he himself had received, and then charge the Twelve with the responsibility of the kingdom of God in all the world. She was present at the Stand on Thursday, August 8, 1844, and delivered her second child, a daughter, one week later. In 1846, they left Nauvoo with the Saints, remained at Council Bluffs for two years, and then proceeded to the Salt Lake Valley, arriving in October, 1849. They settled in Salt Lake City, built a lovely home where she remained while her husband served in St. George and in Washington, D.C., evacuated the city under threat of Johnston's army and returned when the army had settled in Fairfield near Lehi. Her son was killed in 1860 while serving a mission to the Indians. She toured the Church settlements with her husband and other leaders. He died in 1876. Bathsheba was a member of the first Relief Society in Nauvoo, served in Ward and Stake Relief Society presidencies in Utah, served as a Director of the Deseret (later LDS) Hospital, as an ordinance worker in the Endowment House, in the Logan Temple and in the Salt Lake Temple, and for fourteen years as Second Counselor to Zina D. H. Young in the General Relief Society Presidency. On Thursday, October 31, 1901, at the age

Joseph the Prophet. I heard Joseph's voice so plain, and even the different actions or gestures were the same in Brigham Young as in Joseph on the occasion referred to by Bishop Burton tonight. I wish to say that the pictures we see here of the Prophet are not true likenesses. Joseph was a handsome man, and above all he was a noble-appearing man. These pictures do not do him justice, and the best I have seen are little better than caricatures."

Testimony of Samuel Amos Woolley

Samuel Amos Woolley,[112] a native of Pennsylvania, who was raised as a practicing Quaker, who was one in a group of nine missionaries sent to open the work in India in 1852, and served as Bishop of the Salt Lake City 9th Ward for 36 years,

---

of 79, she was called to serve as the fourth General President of the Relief Society. She served in that position until just before her death, at Salt Lake City, on Saturday, September 10, 1910, at the age of 88. (See "*Autobiography* [1822–1906] *of Bathsheba Wilson Bigler Smith 1822–1910*," L. Tom Perry Special Collections, Harold B. Lee Library, Brigham Young University, Provo, Utah and "*Autobiography of Bathsheba W. Smith: Charter Member and Fourth President of Relief Society*" (Ms 267), Marriott Library, University of Utah; compare Jenson, "*Bathsheba W. Smith*," ***LDS Biographical Encyclopedia***, Vol. 1, p. 781.

112. Samuel Amos Woolley's witness of this event is found in Jenson, "*Samuel Amos Woolley*," ***LDS Biographical Encyclopedia***, Vol. 1, p. 781, brackets added.

Samuel Amos Woolley was born in New Lynn, Chester County, Pennsylvania, Sunday, September 11, 1825, a son of John Woolley and Rachel Dilworth. His mother died the following year and his father died in 1832, leaving seven children, ranging in age from Edwin, 25, who was married and is the grandfather of Spencer W. Kimball and J. Reuben Clark, Jr., to Samuel who was seven years old. Under the leadership of his older brother, the children remained together and "raised each other." The Prophet's father lived with the Woolleys for a time to escape the persecutions at Kirtland, and during that period, the Woolley's learned much about the Gospel and were baptized. The family joined the Saints in Nauvoo where

and was a great uncle of President Spencer Woolley Kimball and J. Reuben Clark, Jr., recorded:

"After the martyrdom of Joseph and Hyrum Smith I was present at the important meeting where Pres[ident] Brigham Young first spoke to the Saints of Joseph's death, and I received a testimony that the mantle of Joseph had fallen upon

---

Samuel was one of the "whittling and whistling brigade," obtained work at the stone quarry and was one of the first to quarry stone for the Nauvoo Temple, and served as a "city guard" from 1844 until the Saints left Nauvoo. He was present at the Stand on Thursday, August 8, 1844, ordained a Seventy in 1845, married Catharine Elizabeth Mehring in May of 1846, and that same year crossed the Mississippi and started for the west, traveling with Brigham Young's second company in 1848 to the Salt Lake Valley, where Samuel was assigned with Apostle George A. Smith to settle Iron County in 1851. The following year, he responded to a call to serve a mission to "Hindoostan" (India). He left in October, 1852, departed San Francisco in January, 1853, and arrived in Calcutta in April. Despite trials and little success, he preached in a number of cities in India, departed in August, 1854, arrived in Boston in February, 1855, served as President of the Delaware Conference under John Taylor until April, 1856 while he regained his strength, and finally returned, after an absence of four years, to Salt Lake City, in August, 1856. Back in Utah, he prospered, "by hard work and strict economy, up early and late, while others are in bed asleep," in business, farming, cattle and land. He was the husband of three wives and father of 21 children. He was called to the Bishopric of the Salt Lake City 9th Ward in 1856, served in Echo Canyon during the threat of Johnston's army, established and operated a "bucket and pail factory" in Parowan, conducted business for Brigham Young in the East and returned with a company of Scandinavian emigrants. That same year he was called as "Acting Bishop," and three years later, as fourth Bishop of the 9th Ward and served, with a leave in 1869 to serve a mission to the "states," a total of 36 years. He died in Salt Lake City on Friday, March 23, 1900, at the age of 75. (See Jenson, *"Samuel Amos Woolley,"* ***LDS Biographical Encyclopedia***, Vol. 1, pp. 781–782; compare B. H. Roberts, *"Missions,"* ***Comprehensive History of the Church***, Vol. 4, pp. 72–73; ***Diary of Samuel Amos Woolley***, 21 Volumes, Church Historical Department; Leonard J. Arrington, ***From Quaker to Latter-day Saint: Bishop Edwin D. Woolley*** (Salt Lake City: Deseret Book , 1976), pp. 47–60, 83–85, 132–137, 157–159, 214–236, 361–366, 411–418, 449–454, 472–482; and R. Lanier Britsch, *"Latter-day Saint Mission*

Brigham Young's shoulder, for when he spoke it seemed as if Joseph himself were speaking, his voice and gestures being exactly like those of the martyred Prophet."

Testimony of Lyman Littlefield

Lyman Omer Littlefield, a native of New York and early convert to the Church,[113] who as a young man marched with Zion's Camp, later served a mission to Great Britain, and published as a pioneer author, recorded:

> *"After Mr. Rigdon dismissed his meeting, Apostle Brigham Young arose and called the people to order. There seemed to be felt a general feeling of relief and all gladly kept their seats to listen to the new speaker, who stated very feelingly in substance that it was contrary to his wishes to so soon have to speak upon the matter of choosing a successor to our beloved Brother Joseph Smith, the Prophet, whom God had raised up to establish the great work of the last days. He felt like anointing his head, as did Aaron, and mourning for his brethren for thirty days in sackcloth and ashes, before entering upon the duty then forced upon him. He said Brother Rigdon seemed to be in a hurry about the matter and the course he had taken made it necessary that the people should come to an understanding and find out upon whom the mantle had fallen. The following are some of his memorable*

---

*to India: 1851–1856," **BYU Studies***, Vol. 12, No. 3 [Spring, 1972], pp. 262–278).

113. See footnote #85. Lyman O. Littlefield's testimony is preserved in Littlefield, ***Reminiscences of Latter-day Saints***, pp. 165–166, brackets added.

words [spoken in the afternoon meeting], which will at once be recognized as being characteristic of that great man:

"'There has been much said about President Rigdon being president of the Church, and leading the people, being the head . . . Brother Rigdon has come one thousand six hundred miles to tell you what he wants to do for us. If the people want President Rigdon to lead them they may have him; but I say unto you that the quorum of the Twelve have the keys of the kingdom of God in all the world.

"'The Twelve are appointed by the finger of God. Here is Brigham: have his knees ever faltered? have his lips ever quivered? Here is Heber [C. Kimball] and the rest of the Twelve, an independent body, who have the keys of the priesthood—the keys of the kingdom of God to deliver to all the world. This is true, so help me God. They stand next to Joseph and are as the First Presidency of the Church.'

"He then went to work as a workman understanding his business. He called for the quorums of priesthood to be seated together in order, as much as the circumstances would permit, and then presented the matter under consideration in a manner so plain and convincing that all could readily understand that Joseph's mantle had fallen upon Brigham Young. It was self-evident that the power and influence that had rested upon Brother Joseph in the performance of his official duties, rested upon him. This became at once so satisfactory that he, at that meeting, became the unanimous choice of all present. In other words, the quorum of Twelve Apostles became as the First Presidency of the Church, and Brigham Young being the president of that quorum made him the first representative man, or president of the Church."

Testimony of Helen Mar Kimball Whitney

Helen Mar Kimball Whitney,[114] who was the oldest daughter of President Heber C. Kimball, and who was the mother Orson F. Whitney, a member of the Quorum of the Twelve Apostles, was in her sixteenth year of age when she attended the prayer meeting at the Stand, was attentive to the proceedings and recorded:

> *"The second day after the apostles' return to Nauvoo, President Brigham Young called a special conference to give Elder Rigdon the opportunity to lay his claims before the Church. Meetings were then held in a grove some little distance east of the temple, where a great multitude gathered together, for this day was to decide who was to 'lead Israel,' Sidney Rigdon or the Twelve Apostles. That was a day never to be forgotten. I was among the number that was obliged to stand, it being impossible for half of the congregation to be seated. Mr. Hatch, a young lawyer, whom I had formed acquaintance with at our theater the spring previous, stood by me. We had been on pleasant terms, but lately he had turned Rigdonite, and frequently during that long harangue, he spoke in defense and praise of the speaker, and tried to convince me that he was the right man to lead the Church. He very quickly learned my*

114. Helen Mar Kimball Whitney's testimony is found in *"Scenes and Incidents in Nauvoo,"* ***Woman's Exponent***, Vol. 11 (1882), p. 130. Helen Mar Kimball was born in Mendon, Monroe County, New York, on Wednesday, August 20, 1828. She was the eldest daughter of Heber C. Kimball and Vilate Murray; he was later called to be an Apostle and served as the First Counselor to President Brigham Young. They heard the Gospel in Mendon, and moved to Ohio in October, 1833. She watched her father depart Kirtland with Brigham Young on their mission to

feelings, and how offensive he had made himself. My father was seated there with Brigham and the rest of the Apostles, and I became very indignant, and quite a war of words ensued, neither of us (of course) yielding the point. Not long after this he married one of Rigdon's daughters, which proved to be the only loadstone that attracted him in that direction . . .

"I can bear witness with hundreds of others who stood that day under the sound of Brigham's voice, of the wonderful and startling effect that it had upon us. If Joseph had risen from the dead and stood before them, it could hardly have made a deeper or more lasting impression. It was the very voice of Joseph himself. This was repeatedly spoken of by the Latter-day Saints. And surely it was a most powerful and

---

England. In 1839, when she was eleven years old, she relocated with her father's family to Nauvoo. She was fifteen years old in 1844 and was present in Nauvoo to witness the events which are the subject of this study. She was sealed in plural marriage to the Prophet Joseph Smith, (see *"Proven in Furnace,"* ***Life of Heber C. Kimball***, Chapter 46, p. 328), although there is no evidence that she lived with him as a wife, (see Stanley B. Kimball, *"Heber C. Kimball and Family, the Nauvoo Years— Endowments and Plural Marriage,"* ***BYU Studies***, Vol. 15, No. 4 [Summer, 1975], p. 465), and after the Martyrdom, to Horace Kimball Whitney. She left Nauvoo with the Saints in 1846 but remained at Winter Quarters while her husband journeyed with the first Pioneer company to the Great Salt Lake Valley. Only a short time after his departure, she gave birth to their first child, a daughter, who soon died, in the Spring of 1847. In the course of her own journey to the Valley, the following year, she lost her second child, a son, whom she considered a "little martyr." She arrived in the Valley in 1848. On Sunday, July 1, 1855, Horace and Helen Mar became the parents of Orson F. Whitney, who was called to be a member of the Quorum of the Twelve, Monday, April 9, 1906, (the same day President David O. McKay was called to be an Apostle), and served until his death in 1931. She wrote extensively of events in Nauvoo and Winter Quarters, and of her father's family, notably *"Life Incidents,"* published in serial form in ***Woman's Exponent***, Vols. 9–10 (1880–1881), *"Scenes and Incidents in Nauvoo,"* ***Woman's Exponent***, Vol. 11 (1882–1883), already cited above, *"Travels Beyond the Mississippi,"* ***Woman's Exponent***, Vol. 13 (October 1, 1884), p. 105; and *"Scenes and*

convincing testimony to them that he was the man, instead of Sidney Rigdon, that was destined to become the 'great leader,' and upon whose shoulders the mantle of Joseph had fallen."

Testimony of Jacob Hamblin

Jacob Hamblin,[115] who was born in Ohio, was converted in Wisconsin in 1842 and moved to Nauvoo that same year, and who, in 1856, was ordained by President Brigham Young as an "Apostle to the Lamanites," recalled

---

Incidents at Winter Quarters," ***Woman's Exponent***, Vol. 13 (1885–1886). She died on Friday, November 13, 1896, at Salt Lake City, at the age of 68.

115. Jacob Hamblin's witness is recorded in ***Jacob Hamblin: A Narrative of His Personal Experience as a Frontiersman, Missionary to the Indians, and as an Explorer—Disclosing Interpositions of Providence, Severe Privations, Many Perilous Situations and Remarkable Escapes***, Edited by James A. Little, 2nd Edition (Salt Lake City: Deseret News, 1909), pp. 20–21. This was first published by George Cannon Lambert as Volume 5 in the ***Faith Promoting Series*** (Salt Lake City: Juvenile Instructor Office, 1881).

Jacob Hamblin was born on Friday, April 2, 1819, at Salem, Ashtabula County, Ohio, a son of Isaiah Hamblin and Daphne Haynes. As a young man he moved to Wisconsin. There he was converted and was baptized by Elder Lyman Stoddard on Thursday, March 3, 1842. He moved to Nauvoo, was present at the meeting on Thursday, August 8, 1844. Subsequently, he baptized his own parents at Nauvoo. He departed with members of his family for Utah, arrived Sunday, September 1, 1850, and settled in the Tooele Valley. He eventually had four wives and twenty-four children. At Tooele, in the face of threats by marauding Indians, he lowered his rifle under direction of the Spirit, refusing to shoot, and began his career as an emissary to the Indians. He was called to establish an Indian Mission in Southern Utah in 1854, and settled on the Santa Clara, a tributary to the Virgin River. From there, he conducted missionary excursions among the various tribes, visiting the Moqui villages in Northern Arizona in 1858, the Navajo tribes in Northern Arizona and the present day four corners area beginning in 1860, and various other tribes. He enjoyed the "confidence, friendship, esteem and trust" of President Brigham Young who, on

"On the 8th of August, 1844, I attended a general meeting of the Saints. Elder Rigdon was there, urging his claims to the presidency of the Church. His voice did not sound like the voice of the true shepherd. When he was about to call a vote of the congregation to sustain him as President of the Church, Elders Brigham Young, Parley P. Pratt and Heber C. Kimball stepped into the stand.

"Brigham Young remarked to the congregation: 'I will manage this voting for Elder Rigdon. He does not preside here. This child' (meaning himself) 'will manage this flock for a season.' The voice and gestures of the man were those of the Prophet Joseph.

"The people, with few exceptions, visibly saw that the mantle of the Prophet Joseph Smith had fallen upon Brigham Young. To some it seemed as though Joseph again stood before them.

"I arose to my feet and said to a man sitting by me, 'That is the voice of the true shepherd—the chief of the Apostles.'"

Friday, December 15, 1876, ordained him to serve as an "Apostle to the Lamanites," a position that he held until his death. In his forty years of service as an emissary to the Indians, he encountered dangers, but never killed an enemy, choosing instead to negotiate and to persuade. The Indians explained their trust in him by stating that "Jacob never lies." Near the end of Jacob's life, Professor H. A. Thompson of the United States Geological Survey said, "I would trust my money, my life and my honor in the keeping of Jacob Hamblin, knowing all would be safe." He moved from Santa Clara to Kanab, Utah in 1870, to Amity, Arizona in 1878, and to Pleasanton, New Mexico in 1882, where he died on Tuesday, August 31, 1886, at the age of 67. When the community of Pleasanton was abandoned, his brother moved his remains to Alpine, Arizona, where the Church erected a monument to his memory, with the inscription: "Peacemaker in the Camp of the Lamanites; Herald of Truth to the House of Israel." (See Andrew Jenson, *"Jacob Hamblin,"* ***LDS Biographical Encyclopedia***, Vol. 3, pp. 100–101).

Testimony of Jane Snyder Richards

Jane Snyder Richards, who was born in New York state, who joined the Church there and migrated to Nauvoo, and who later served as First Counselor in the General Relief Society Presidency,[116] recalled:

> *"After his tragic death I attended the meeting at which President Brigham Young addressed the Saints, and saw his face illuminated and appear as the face of Joseph while the voice of Joseph seemed to address the people through the mouth of Brigham. I can never forget the divine thrill that passed through the audience on that occasion and the impression that the appearance and voice of Joseph produced upon his hearers."*

---

116. Jane Snyder Richards's testimony was printed in *"Joseph Smith," **The Young Women's Journal**,* Vol. 16 (1905), p. 550. Jane Richards was born on Friday, January 31, 1823, in Pamelia, New York, a daughter of Isaac Richards and Lovise Comstock Snyder. She joined the Church there and relocated with members of her family to Nauvoo where she became the wife of Franklin Dewey Richards, on Sunday, December 18, 1842. She was a member of the first Relief Society that was established by the Prophet Joseph Smith in Nauvoo, attended the meetings at the Stand on Thursday, August 8, 1844, sustained the Twelve Apostles with Brigham Young at their head as the leaders of the Church, remained in Nauvoo until the "exodus" in 1846, and ultimately, while her husband served a mission to England, journeyed west with the Saints, suffering first from the death of her infant son, then from the death of her daughter—their only children, and from almost constant illness herself. She stopped for a year at Winter Quarters where she was finally reunited with her husband, and they then traveled with the Saints to the Salt Lake Valley, arriving on Thursday, October 19, 1848. Her husband served as a judge, was called to be an Apostle in 1849, and served from Tuesday, September 13, 1898 until his death the following year as President of the Quorum of the Twelve. She was the mother of six children. The Richards family established permanent residence in Ogden, Weber County, Utah, in 1869. There she organized the Relief Society and was called to be the first president of the Weber Stake Relief Society, organized on Thursday, July 19, 1877, by President Brigham Young, a

Testimony of Lewis Barney

Lewis Barney,[117] a native of New York who joined the Church in Iowa during the Nauvoo period, who was faithful and diligent in support of the Prophet Joseph Smith, and who was one of the original Pioneer company in July, 1847, testified

> *". . . the Saints, after the loss of their beloved Prophet, were somewhat thrown into confusion, not having the necessary experience to enable them to know and understand who to look to for a leader, and would gather together . . . and consult with each other as to who should be the leader of the Church. Reflections of a serious nature were in everyone's mind, some saying the best we can do is to stick to the biggest lump. In the meantime, as soon as Sidney Rigdon heard the tidings of the death of the Prophet, with all speed left Pittsburgh, Pennsylvania, and came flying on the cars to Nauvoo, gathered the weeping Saints to lay before them the necessity of choosing a guardian to take care of them until they should come of age, saying, 'you are now 14 years old, and have the privilege to choose a guardian to*

---

position that she held for thirty-one years. She served as a member of the Relief Society General Board during this period, and from 1888 to 1901, she served concurrently as Stake Relief Society President and as First Counselor in the Relief Society General Presidency to Zina Diantha Young. She was one of Utah's representatives to the National Council of Women in 1891, when the Relief Society and Young Women's Mutual Improvement Association became affiliated with that organization. She was also vice president of the Utah Board of Lady Managers of the World's Fair at Chicago, Illinois, in 1893. She died on Sunday, November 17, 1912, in Ogden, at the age of 89.

117. Lewis Barney's record of the mantle of the Prophet Joseph Smith falling upon Brigham Young is found in his, "***Reminiscences,***" (ca. 1886–1888),

look after the interests of the Church.' It seemed the majority of the Saints had forgotten or overlooked the time the Prophet, in the presence of the whole body of Saints, in time of Conference, took hold of his coat with both hands and shook himself all over from head to foot, saying, 'I this day shake Sidney Rigdon off of my shoulders as my Counselor. He is no more my counselor. I will carry him no longer, but if the Church wishes to carry him, they can do so.' Sidney Rigdon held two or three meetings, and got all things ready for a vote to be called to see if the Saints were willing to sustain him as their guardian. Parley P. Pratt, one of the Twelve, was busy working in his garden, and paid little or no attention to Sidney Rigdon until he was notified that Sidney was about to call a vote of the Saints to manifest their feelings in relation to his being their guardian. Parley, on receiving this information, dropped his hoe and came to the meeting, walked on the Stand barefoot, his pants rolled up above his ankles, and his short sleeves half way to his elbows, soon put a stop to the plan Sidney was laying to ensnare the Saints.

The next day, President Brigham Young arrived in Nauvoo with some of the other Apostles from a mission to the eastern States and called a meeting . . . President Young then arose and took the Stand, his face and countenance having the appearance of Joseph, his voice and words were the familiar voice and words of our martyred Prophet, so much so [that]

Church Historical Department, Salt Lake City, Utah, pp. 13–17; editor's note: "Spelling and capitalization have been modified in this narrative to conform to current usage, and punctuation has been added." Lewis Barney was born in New York State, Thursday, September 8, 1808. His father, Charles Barney, moved his family to Knox County, Ohio, when Lewis was three years old. While

the whole congregation was fully satisfied that the Mantle of the Prophet Joseph had fallen on him; and some of the Saints really believed it was in reality the Prophet himself. Well do I remember the feelings that possessed my breast at that time. I knew it was Brigham Young, and being familiar with the countenance, voice and the manner of the speech of the Prophet Joseph Smith, I also knew the mantle of the Prophet had fallen on Brigham, and it was marvelous, and the miracle wrought by the power of God in the sight and hearing of the whole multitude, that they might never doubt that Brigham

---

in Ohio, his father served in the United States Army in the War of 1812 against England. The Barney's farmed in Ohio until 1825. In that year, his father secured a soldier's patent right to 160 acres in Spoon River, Illinois, but his mother died just as the family made preparations to move to Illinois, and so the younger children were left with relatives, and Lewis and his brother accompanied their father to Illinois where they established farms and then returned for the younger children. He married Elizabeth Turner in 1832, served in the United States Army in the Blackhawk War, and farmed. In 1838, Lewis and his father both sold their farms in Illinois and moved to Iowa where they established farms. He investigated the Church for a year and half, and finding that the Latter-day Saints were "honest, industrious, and wickedly misrepresented," was baptized in the Mississippi River in 1840 by Alva Tippits and confirmed by the Prophet Joseph. They sold their farms and moved to Nauvoo in 1841. At one point, he loaned the Prophet $200 for which he received the Prophet's note due in six months. Not long after, the Prophet was murdered, and under threat of the mob Lewis was forced to abandon his farm and move within the city of Nauvoo. On February 7, 1846, he used his means to remove the poor of the city from Nauvoo. They camped at Sugar Creek, and then moved west. He wrote: "At the end of three weeks we rolled out and set our faces westward trusting in the providences of Almighty God for our deliverance. On reaching the summit between the Mississippi and Des Moines Rivers the company made a halt for the purpose of taking a last and peering look at the Nauvoo Temple, the spire of which was then glittering in the bright shining sun. The last view of the temple was witnessed in the midst of sighs and lamentations, all faces in gloom and sorrow bathed in tears, at being forced from our homes and Temple that had cost so much toil and suffering to complete its erection," (Lewis Barney,

was the chosen leader of the Church. Having this assurance, the Saints were prepared to pay strict heed to his counsel. In his opening remarks, he said, 'There seems to be a manifest feeling to hurry things. If I had been here, I would set apart 30 days for mourning for the loss of our beloved Prophet, after which I would have paid my attention to set in order the affairs of the Church. Sidney Rigdon is not the man to lead this Church. I am the man God has chosen. You think I dare not say it but I dare, and now my throat is ready for the knife,' at the same time drawing his hand across his throat. At the close of the meeting, Sidney took passage on board a steam boat and floated off down the Mississippi River, and has not been known among the Saints since. Brigham Young together with the Twelve, directed their attention to the finishing the Temple which, at the time of the death of the Prophet, was up to middle of the first rows of windows. The Saints, having settled down in their feelings, were willing to take hold of the work with renewed diligence. The Temple was pushed forward as fast as possible [as they] united themselves under the direction of President Brigham Young . . ."

"*Autobiography*," Typescript, L. Tom Perry Special Collections, Harold B. Lee Library, Brigham Young University, Provo, Utah, p. 28). He was chosen as one of the twelve twelves and served as a teamster in the journey to the Valley of the Great Salt Lake with the Pioneer company in 1847. He returned that same year to Kanesville, Iowa, established a farm and remained there until 1852, and then moved his family to Utah, where he settled in what is now Utah County, and subsequently in Manti, and even contemplated settling in Bowie, Arizona and Mancos, Colorado. He was involved in the Indian wars in Utah, was part of the United Order in Monroe, Utah, and labored diligently to redeem his kindred dead and to secure a common home for his posterity. He died Monday, November 5, 1894, at Mancos, Colorado. Compare Ronald O. Barney, ***One Side By Himself: The Life and Times of Lewis Barney*** (Logan, Utah: Utah State University Press, 2001).

Testimony of Mary Ann Sterns Winters

Mary Ann Sterns Winters,[118] because she was the stepdaughter of Elder Parley P. Pratt, enjoyed a close association with the Prophet's family in Nauvoo. She was ten years old when she attended the meeting at the Stand in Nauvoo on Thursday, August 8, 1844, and recorded:

> *". . . those awful days came that terminated in the martyrdom of Brother Joseph and Hyrum Smith, and oh, the horror and gloom and heartaches and trials of those days. The very atmosphere was so oppressive that it seemed difficult to breathe. Everything seemed to stand still and with such an awful stillness and everyone seemed looking to another for some help, and to know what to do in their awful extremity. Many imagined that Brother Joseph's life could not be taken and the shock to them was doubly great, and all were looking for a message from somewhere, and it came in due time. Our Prophet and Patriarch were gone, and the weight of the Church rested on the body of the Church, and right bravely and unflinchingly did they hold it for the time being, faithfully trusting in the promise that God's kingdom had come to stay, and would not be broken up, though the headlight was obscured and the darkness was profound.*

---

118. Mary Ann Sterns Winters, "*Autobiography 1833–1853*," Typescript, Church Historical Department, Salt Lake City, Chapter 14, p. 1. Mary Ann Sterns Winters was born in Maine in 1833. Her father died soon thereafter, and her mother joined the Church in 1836 and relocated to Kirtland to be near the Saints. She attended many meetings in the Kirtland Temple as a child, and at Kirtland, her mother was married to Elder Parley P. Pratt, and she became a stepdaughter to Elder Parley P. Pratt. She traveled with him and his family on a mission to

"Brother [Parley P.] Pratt on his mission in the eastern states was impressed by the Holy Spirit to return home to Nauvoo . . . He hastened onward, and a few days later, just as the sun appeared over the eastern prairies, he . . . opened the door and walked into the dining room unannounced and unlooked for, the surprise being like an electric shock, and truly he brought the sunlight of the Holy Spirit with him—faith, hope, courage and strength—cheer to press onward undaunted. The burden seemed lifted, for he came with the power of the Holy Priesthood, and the light of revelation that had been given him for the occasion, and the hearts of the faithful turned from their sorrow to the upholding and sustaining of the work that our beloved Prophet and Patriarch had laid down their lives as a sacrifice for. Each day as he met in council with Brothers Richards and Taylor, he brought us fresh words of encouragement, and soon Brother Brigham, Brother Kimball and the others arrived, each filled with the spirit of their calling and were a mighty phalanx in the cause of righteousness, and through the gloom could be plainly felt, the rod of iron was there, and the majority took strong hold and walked firmly on even unto the end of their days on earth.

"I was at the great meeting when the mantle of Brother Joseph rested upon Brigham Young until his whole being seemed changed and his voice was like that of the Prophet.

England, returning to Nauvoo in April, 1843 via steamboat from New Orleans. As a young girl, she sang in the choir at the Temple block in 1843. She recalled that she "stood close by the Prophet while he was preaching . . . in the grove by the temple," and testified that "the Holy Spirit lighted up his countenance till it glowed like a halo around him, and his words penetrated the hearts of all who heard him." ("*Joseph Smith,*" ***The Young Woman's Journal***, Vol. 16 [1905], p. 558). The family of Parley P. Pratt lived in Nauvoo when the Martyrdom occurred;

The people around me, rising to their feet to get a better chance to hear and see, I and my little companion of the day, Julia Felshaw, being small of stature, stood upon the benches that we, too might behold the wonderful transformation, and I know that from that time on the power of that change remained with Brother Brigham Young as long as he lived on earth.

"The faithful and honest hearted were quick to discern the right and took up the armor of the gospel anew, rallied around the faithful Brigham whose rightful leadership had been plainly shown to them, and went to work with renewed zeal to whatever he pointed out to do. The temple was hurried on to completion. The songs of the earnest workers as they tugged at the ropes, pulling up the heavy stones to the top of the building were cheering and inspiring as they floated out on the morning air and all seemed to work with a new interest at whatever the duties of the day called forth, thus fulfilling the saying that the blood of the martyrs is the seed of the Church."

Mary Ann viewed the bodies of the Prophet Joseph and Hyrum as they lay in state at the Mansion House, and was present at the meetings on Thursday, August 8, 1844. In 1852, she traveled to the Salt Lake Valley. In time, Mary Ann married Oscar Winters, they settled in Pleasant Grove, Utah, where she became a school teacher and the mother of eight children, including Augusta Winters Grant, her second daughter, who became the wife of President Heber J. Grant. Her stepfather was killed by an assassin's bullet on Wednesday, May 13, 1857, in Van Buren, Crawford County, Arkansas, leaving an extensive family without a head; his eldest son, Parley Parker Pratt was only twenty years old—Mary Ann was 24 at the time. In 1885, with her daughter Augusta, she traveled east to visit her childhood home in Bethel, Maine. She died on Tuesday, April 2, 1912, in Salt Lake City. Her record of the valor of early Latter-day Saint women was published after her death, under the title *"Mothers in Israel: The Nauvoo Battle,"* in ***The Relief Society Magazine***, Vol. 4 (February, 1917), pp. 79–82.

Testimony of Wilford Woodruff

Wilford Woodruff,[119] himself an eyewitness to this transformation of Brigham Young, and at the time ranked fourth in seniority in the Quorum, after Orson Hyde, Orson Pratt, and John Taylor, explained the Lord's purpose:

> *"I know this work is of God. I know Joseph Smith was a Prophet of God. I have heard two or three of the brethren testify about Brother Young in Nauvoo. Every man and every woman in that assembly, which perhaps might number thousands, could bear the same testimony. I was there, the Twelve were there, and a good many others, and all can bear the same testimony. The question might be asked, 'why was the appearance of Joseph Smith given to Brigham Young?' Because here was Sidney Rigdon and other men rising up and claiming to be the leaders of the Church, and men stood, as it were, on a pivot, not knowing which way to turn. But just as quick as Brigham Young rose in that assembly, his face was that of Joseph Smith—the mantle of Joseph had fallen upon him, the power of God that was upon Joseph Smith was upon him, he had the voice of Joseph, and it was the voice of the shepherd. There was not a person in that assembly, Rigdon, himself, not excepted, but was satisfied in his own mind that Brigham was the proper leader of the people, for he [Sidney Rigdon] would not have his name presented [for vote*

---

119. Wilford Woodruff's testimony, as cited here, was part of an address entitled *"Comprehensiveness of Latter-day Work,"* presented at the 42nd Annual General Conference, in the Tabernacle in Salt Lake City, Monday, April 8, 1872, reported by David W. Evans, in ***Journal of Discourses***, Vol. 15, pp. 80–81, brackets added).

in the afternoon meeting], by his own consent, after that sermon was delivered. There was a reason for this in the mind of God; it convinced the people. They saw and heard for themselves, and it was by the power of God."

Testimony of George Q. Cannon

In 1884, George Q. Cannon,[120] who had served as Counselor in the First Presidency to President Brigham Young, and would later serve as First Counselor to President Wilford Woodruff and First Counselor to President Lorenzo Snow, but who, at the time of this writing, was serving as First Counselor to President John Taylor, testified:

---

120. President George Q. Cannon, *"God Confirms the Authority of His Servants by Manifestations of His Power and Favor,"* an address in the Tabernacle in Salt Lake City, Sunday, December 14, 1884, reported by John Irvine, ***Journal of Discourses***, Vol. 26, pp. 60–61.

George Q. Cannon was born in Liverpool, England on Thursday, January 11, 1827. His parents were introduced to the Gospel through the missionary efforts of John Taylor in 1840, and shortly thereafter, he was baptized. The family removed to Nauvoo in 1843, where he entered the printing and publishing office of John Taylor, who had become his uncle by marriage, and who he would later serve as First Counselor in the First Presidency. He was seventeen years old in 1844 and was present in the meeting at the Stand on Thursday, August 8, 1844, and offered fervent testimony throughout the remainder of his life that the "mantle" of the Prophet Joseph Smith fell up Brigham Young in a miraculous and marvelous manner at that meeting. He left Nauvoo in the early Spring of 1846, remained with the main body of the Saints at Winter Quarters, and traveled to Utah with the family of John Taylor, arriving in the Salt Lake Valley on Sunday, October 3, 1847. Two years later he went to California in company with Elder Charles C. Rich, and the next year was called with nine others on a mission to the Hawaiian Islands. On returning from that mission he was appointed to labor in California, where he founded and published the *Western Standard*, a Church newspaper that issued in 1856 and 1857. He was ordained an Apostle on Sunday, August 26, 1860,

"And when Joseph was taken, how was it then? Were the people left without some man or men to stand up in their midst to declare to them the counsel of their Almighty Father? No, the Lord did not leave His people without a shepherd. He had anticipated the dreadful tragedy which would rob us of His anointed one; rob us, the Church of Christ, of our Prophet and Patriarch . . . and previous to this horrid tragedy, He inspired His servant Joseph to call other men, upon whom He bestowed all the keys, all the authority, all the blessings, all the knowledge so far as endowments were concerned, so far as the power to go unto God and ask Him in the name of Jesus, and obtain His mind and will, was concerned. He bestowed upon these men the same gifts, and blessings, and graces, he had received; so that there was a body of men with all the authority, a body of prophets with all the gifts of seers and revelators . . . and the earth was not robbed of that Priesthood which God had sent His angels from heaven to restore once more to the children of men and to act on the earth in the plenitude of its power. There was no more need, therefore, for angelic visitation to restore it. It was not taken back to God by the slaying of the Prophet and Patriarch, but remained with mortal man here on the earth. And, then, when the question arose as to who should lead

---

at the age of 33. He founded, owned, edited and published ***The Juvenile Instructor***, which began publication in January, 1866, the first children's magazine published between the Mississippi River and the West Coast of the United States. (President Cannon presented the magazine to the Church in 1901 and the magazine continued in various formats until 1970). In the course of his editorship, he diligently sought out the Saints who had known the Prophet Joseph Smith personally, solicited their written reflections and testimonies about the Prophet, and published them. He was called as Counselor to President Young in 1873, as the First Counselor to President John Taylor in 1880, as First Counselor to President Wilford Woodruff in 1889, and as First Counselor to President Lorenzo Snow in

Israel, notwithstanding Sidney Rigdon stood up in the congregation of the Saints, and plead for the leadership of the people, the spirit and power of the Almighty descended upon the man whom God had chosen to hold the keys. In the midst of all Israel, in the face of the entire congregation of believers and unbelievers, God clothed His servant with such power and in such a manner that every man that had the least portion of the spirit of God, and every woman, knew by the manifestations of that spirit, and by the outpouring of the gift of God upon that man, that he was the chosen one, and that upon him rested the authority, and the power, and the gifts that had been borne by the Prophet Joseph during his lifetime. No more plainly was the power of God manifested in behalf of Elisha, after the taking away of Elijah, than it was manifested in behalf of President Brigham Young, when the Prophet Joseph was taken from the earth, and from that day, while he lived on the earth until he died, the Lord magnified him in the eyes of the people and blessed those who listened to his counsel."

Testimony of William Lampard Watkins

William L. Watkins,[121] who was born in England, joined the Church there in 1842, relocated with his father's family to Nauvoo, and served a mission to Kentucky, in May and June of 1844, to advance the political candidacy of the Prophet Joseph Smith. He testified:

1898. He died at Monterey, California, on Friday, April 12, 1901, at the age of 74.

121. William Lampard Watkins's witness was first published in his "*Autobiography 1827–1846,*" Typescript, L. Tom Perry Special Collections, in the

"... one day near Georgetown I became perfectly dark in my mind and quite discouraged. I sought to overcome this feeling by calling on the Lord for help, but could not continue. As it were, a voice made an impression on my mind to go to Cincinnati. A boat had just come up the river and docked. I stepped on board and the first person I met was Elder George J. Adams. Being very well acquainted with him I told him freely of my feelings. He said, 'Brother William, I have sorrowful news. Our Prophet and our Patriarch were murdered in Carthage Jail ...' The same day I got on a boat and went to St. Louis and from there took boat to Nauvoo. It was a serious and trying time. Few of the elders had yet arrived and the condition of the Saints was mournful in the extreme. Our enemies were rejoicing in what had been done, yet full of fear. History, of course, gives a full account of these perilous times.

"Sidney Rigdon, one of Joseph Smith's Counselors who had gone to Pittsburgh, hastened home on hearing of the martyrdom of the Prophet and with some of his friends sought to influence the people to appoint him as guardian to build up the church to Joseph, but few of the Twelve had arrived and John Taylor was suffering from the wounds he had received at the time of the martyrdom.

Harold B. Lee Library, Brigham Young University, p. 3. William Lampard Watkins was born in Islington, London, Middlesex, England, on Wednesday, February 7, 1827, the son of William Watkins and Hannah Lampard. He was the first of his father's family to join the Church, and was baptized in London in 1842 by James Albon and confirmed by Lorenzo Snow. In October, 1842, the family shipped from Liverpool aboard the *Emerald* with a company of Saints led by Elder Parley P. Pratt to New Orleans, and then by the river steamer *Goddess of Liberty* to Nauvoo. At the General Conference of the Church, in April of 1844, William was appointed to serve a mission in Kentucky, to preach the gospel and to advance the political candidacy of the Prophet, and he departed for Kentucky, but after

"A meeting was appointed for August 8th by which time Brigham Young and most of the other apostles had returned home. It was at this meeting Sidney Rigdon made a lengthy and tedious speech presenting his claims, telling the people what wonderful things he had planned for them. It was a solemn time, for he was a man who on account of his experience and talents had been sustained as Joseph's counselor by the people, although contrary to the Prophet's wish for some time past, but the darkness was soon dispelled, for Brigham Young explained before the people on that day, the order of the Priesthood. He was filled with the power of the Holy Ghost. He stood before the people as the Prophet Joseph Smith often had done and we heard the voice of the true shepherd, for he spoke with the voice of Joseph. His manner and appearance were like unto Joseph's and it was manifested to all those present upon whom the responsibility rested to carry on the work of God and lead the Saints.

"I sat in that assembly and did not realize for a time but that I was still listening to the Prophet Joseph, so great and marvelous was the manner in which the manifestation before the entire congregation was made, that when the proposition

---

hearing news of the Martyrdom, he returned to Nauvoo and was present to witness the divine manifestation poured out upon the Saints at the close of the prayer meeting on Thursday, August 8, 1844. He married two wives in plural marriage, and was appointed to be a member of the sixth quorum of the Seventy at Nauvoo. He left Nauvoo with the main body of the Saints, and with his family, in the early Spring of 1846, and journeyed first to Winter Quarters, and then to the Salt Lake Valley, arriving in Utah in 1852. He remained in Salt Lake City until 1861, then settled in Box Elder County where he taught school, served for thirty years as secretary and treasurer of the Brigham City Mercantile and Manufacturing Association, served as a counselor in the Box Elder Stake Presidency to President Rudger Clawson for twenty years, and was ordained a Patriarch by President Lorenzo Snow and served from Saturday, November 7,

was placed before the people to decide whom they would sustain as the leader of the Church, the Twelve Apostles with Brigham Young as their president were almost unanimously sustained. This circumstance, although the Saints were in deep trouble and filled with sorrow for the condition in which they were placed brought a great relief and gave joy to the Saints for they realized that God was still mindful of them."

Testimony of George Romney

In one of the last public testimonies that the mantle of the Prophet Joseph Smith visibly fell upon Brigham Young, offered by one who could speak with certainty as an eyewitness to the event, delivered in a Fast and Testimony meeting convened for all Temple workers in the Salt Lake Temple, on Sunday, January 6, 1918, George Romney[122], in the 87th year of his life, declared:

It is a little over seventy-eight years, now, since I was baptized a member of The Church of Jesus Christ of Latter-day Saints . . . In the year 1841 we arrived in the city of Nauvoo,

---

1896 until his death in Brigham City, Monday, September 18, 1911. He is the great grandfather to William Mack Watkins who served as First Counselor in the Crestwood (Kaysville Utah) Stake Presidency, 1989–1997, and as President of the Czech Republic Prague Mission, 1998–2001.

122. From *"A Testimony"* presented in the Salt Lake Temple "fast and testimony meeting," Sunday, January 6, 1918. Under the urging and direction of President Joseph F. Smith, this testimony of George Romney was transcribed, and published in ***The Improvement Era***, Vol. 21, No. 8 (June 1918), pp. 752–753.

George Romney was born in Dalton, Lancashire, England, on Sunday, August 14, 1831. He moved with his family to Preston in 1833 where his parents

having crossed the ocean on the ship. I remember well when the boat landed there. It took three weeks to go up from New Orleans to Nauvoo. We were met there by the Prophet Joseph and some others, to welcome us there, just a short time after they had been driven from Missouri. It was a sickly place. About one-third of our shipload died inside of three weeks . . .

"The Prophet Joseph . . . and Brigham Young . . . were men of God. I want to tell a little about these things, because there are not many left who can do it. When the Prophet Joseph and his brother Hyrum, the Patriarch, were killed, John Taylor, who was severely wounded, and Willard Richards, came home. Then Strang and others arose, even Sidney Rigdon, and they each said: 'I am the leader of this people;' and they would talk to us, and did talk for two or three months, until the Twelve returned from the East to Nauvoo. Then a meeting was called, and Sidney Rigdon got

---

were baptized in 1839 and he was baptized soon after. The family left England in 1841, sailing on the *Sheffield*, the first ship carrying English converts to America, and settled in Nauvoo where George learned the carpenter's trade and served as an apprentice during construction of the Nauvoo Temple. He was present at the assembly on Thursday, August 8, 1844. When the Saints left Nauvoo, the Romneys stopped in Burlington, Iowa, later moved to St. Louis to find work to procure ox teams, and finally made the trek to the Salt Lake Valley, arriving in October, 1850. George, now nineteen, had met and married Jane Jamison in St. Louis, and their first child was born soon after their arrival in the Valley, in a wagon box on what is now Temple square. Eventually he became husband and father to a large family. In Utah, he obtained employment as a carpenter on the public works, where he assisted with the construction of the capitol building in Fillmore, served as a captain in Echo Canyon during the resistance to Johnston's army, and eventually became carpenter foreman on public works, where he served until 1864. With William H. Folsom, he formed a construction company that built the first Salt Lake City Hall, the Wells Fargo building, a number of other large buildings in the city, and many private homes. In 1868, he joined with two others to form Taylor, Romney, Armstrong & Co., a timber and milling enterprise,

up and spoke. Of course, he was a man of eloquence, a man who had studied rhetoric and everything that pertains to being a speaker. He talked for one hour and a half. Then Brigham Young got up, and I want to testify to you, in all soberness, this morning, that the mantle of Joseph fell upon Brigham, and his voice was as the voice of Joseph Smith. This, my brethren and sisters, I testify to you in the name of the Lord God of Israel. I saw it and I heard his voice."

The Mantle Remains—The Witness Continues

Emmeline B. Wells,[123] a native of Massachusetts, was baptized at the age of fourteen, buried her first child in Nauvoo, lost her husband, buried her mother in Iowa and her second husband shortly after their arrival in the Salt Lake Valley. She became an accomplished writer and served as editor of the *Woman's Exponent*—a paper that was owned and published by Mormon women, and that was eventually replaced by the

which prospered. Eventually he was elected to the city council, and also served as an officer or director in a number of enterprises including ZCMI, Home Fire Insurance, Deseret National Bank, Deseret Savings Bank, Consolidated Wagon and Machine Company; Clark, Eldredge & Company, Alberta Land and Cattle Company and Utah Power and Light. He served a number of missions, one to England and several within the States, served a brief term in the penitentiary with other brethren during the Edmunds persecutions, and in 1888, was sustained as Bishop of the Salt Lake 20th Ward where he served for many years. After dedication of the Salt Lake Temple, he became a Temple worker, and continued active in his business activities and temple service until his death, on Sunday, February 1, 1920, in Salt Lake City, at the age of 89. (Andrew Jenson, *"George Romney,"* ***LDS Biographical Encyclopedia***, Vol. 1, p. 678).

123. Emmeline Blanche Woodward Wells was born Friday, February 29, 1828 at Petersham, Worchester County, Massachusetts. She was baptized Tuesday,

Relief Society Magazine. She served as the fifth General President of the Relief Society. To her, the Lord's chosen servant—the Prophet Joseph Smith, who possessed the mantle of authority and power, seemed "transfigured" and was "beyond comprehension."[124]

March 1, 1842 at the age of fourteen; married the following year and relocated with her husband and widowed mother and siblings to Nauvoo where she first met the Prophet in April 1844 and heard his last public sermons that fateful Spring. After the martyrdom, her husband's family left the Church. She was present on Thurday, August 8, 1844, when the mantle of the Prophet Joseph Smith fell upon Brigham Young. A month later, her first child was born, a son that died, and thereafter her husband left her. She left Nauvoo, buried her mother in Iowa, and journeyed with her younger siblings to Winter Quarters where she was sealed in plural marriage to Bishop Newell K. Whitney, and following his death, to Daniel H. Wells who became a Counselor to President Brigham Young. She served as editor of the ***Women's Exponent*** from 1874 until 1914—a period of forty years, and as the fifth General President of the Relief Society from 1910 until 1921. She was active in the suffrage movement, eventually serving as a delegate to the Women's International Council and Congress in London in 1899 and was the first western woman elected as an officer in the Woman's National Council. She died in Salt Lake City on Monday, April 25, 1921, at the age of 93. (See Andrew Jenson, *"Emmeline Blanche Woodward Wells,"* ***LDS Biographical Encyclopedia,*** Vol. 2, pp. 731–34).

124. It must be remembered that the mantle which fell that day upon Brigham Young first rested upon the Prophet Joseph Smith. Emmeline Blanche Woodward Wells recalled her impressions upon meeting the Prophet, when she first arrived in Nauvoo, in April 1844, and of the power that appeared to rest upon him in all of his sermons and ministrations to the Saints:

> "Journeying from . . . Massachusetts to Nauvoo, Illinois, with a company of Latter-day Saints, we . . . joined . . . elders returning from missions in the eastern states . . . ***I listened carefully to all the elders' conversation*** for they were full of zeal and the spirit of the Latter-day work; and of ***love for the Prophet Joseph. To me it was a continuous revelation*** . . .
>
> "As we neared our destination . . . the elders . . . were full of enthusiasm at the thought of seeing the Prophet again. But ***not once in all the conversation did I hear a description of his personal appearance. There were no photographs in those days . . .***

Her statement underscores the fundamental principle of the Lord's provision for succession in the leadership of the Church: he may be a good man, even a great man, he may be a man possessed of gifts, extraordinary talents and abilities; he may even be an Apostle, perhaps even a Prophet. But the "mantle" will "transfigure" the man. He will then be "the Prophet," and he will be equal to all the challenges before him,

---

"At last the boat reached the upper landing, and a crowd of people were coming toward the bank of the river. As we stepped ashore the crowd advanced, and ***I could see one person who towered away and above all the others around him; in fact I did not see distinctly any others. His majestic bearing, so entirely different from anyone I had ever seen . . . was more than a surprise. It was as if I beheld a vision; I seemed to be lifted off my feet, to be as it were walking in the air, and paying no heed whatever to those around me.*** I made my way through the crowd, then I saw this man whom I had noticed, because of his lofty appearance, shaking hands with all the people, men, women and children. Before I was aware of it he came to me, and ***when he took my hand, I was simply electrified,—thrilled through and through to the tips of my fingers, and every part of my body . . . I am sure that for a few minutes I was not conscious of motion. I think I stood still, I did not want to speak, or be spoken to. I was overwhelmed with indefinable emotion . . .***

"The one thought that filled my soul was, I have seen the Prophet of God, he has taken me by the hand, and this testimony has never left me in all the 'perils by the way.' It is as vivid today as ever it was. For many years, I felt it too sacred an experience even to mention.

It was my good fortune to go immediately on my arrival to a home where the Prophet Joseph was almost idolized, and I heard of the wonderful power he possessed, and everything concerning him it was possible to learn.

"I heard him preach all his last sermons, and frequently met him and shook hands with him, and always felt in my inmost soul, he is indeed a man unlike all others.

"In the Prophet Joseph Smith . . . I recognized the great spiritual power that brought joy and comfort to the Saints . . . that strong comradeship that made such a bond of brotherliness with those who were

whatever the task, whatever the obstacles. With the "mantle" resting upon him, he will surely be enabled to "go," as Nephi noted long ages ago "and do the things which the Lord hath commanded."[125] The Lord had declared to His servant Moses, on the eve of his prophetic mission to lead ancient Israel out of bondage and to make of them a holy people, that

> *"I am the God of thy father, the God of Abraham, the God of Isaac, and the God of Jacob . . .*
>
> *"I will send thee . . .*
>
> *"Certainly I will be with thee . . .*
>
> *"Now therefore go, and I will be with thy mouth, and teach thee what thou shalt say."*[126]

---

his companions . . . in which he reached men's souls, and appealed most forcibly to their friendship and loyalty. He possessed too the innate refinement that one finds in the born poet . . . ***this extraordinary temperament and force combined is something of a miracle*** . . .

*"**He was beyond my comprehension. The power of God rested upon him to such a degree that on many occasions he seemed transfigured.*** His expression was mild and almost child-like in repose; and ***when addressing the people, the glory of his countenance was beyond description.*** At other times the great power of his manner, more than of his voice . . . seemed to shake the place on which we stood and penetrate the inmost soul of his hearers, and I am sure that then they would have laid down their lives to defend him. I always listened spell-bound to his every utterance—the chosen of God in this last dispensation." (*"Recollections of Joseph Smith,"* ***Young Woman's Journal***, Vol. 16 [1905], pp. 554–555).

125. The Prophet Nephi, son of Lehi, as part of his record of the inaugural events of the Nephite dispensation, probably written near the close of his own ministry, "forty years" after "the time" that Lehi and his family "left Jerusalem," approximately 559–545 B.C., in 1 Nephi 3:7.

126. Exodus 3:6, 12; 4:12. Compare 1 Nephi 17; 22:20; 2 Nephi 3; Helaman 8:11–13; D&C 8:3; 28:1–7; 84:23–25; 103:16; 133:63.

The Lord has made very clear that He will be with His servants, that they will never, not ever, be without Him:

> *". . . the duty of the President of the office of the High Priesthood is to preside over the whole church, and to be like unto Moses—*
>
> *". . . yea, to be a seer, a revelator, a translator, and a prophet, having all the gifts of God which he bestows upon the head of the church."*[127]
>
> *". . . whoso receiveth you, there I will be also, for I will go before your face. I will be on your right hand and on your left, and my Spirit shall be in your hearts, and mine angels round about you, to bear you up. [And] whoso receiveth you receiveth me;"*[128]

The Lord had instructed His servants in an earlier age, and reiterated the same principles, and commandment and warning, in this age:

> *"He that heareth you heareth me; and he that despiseth you despiseth me; and he that despiseth me despiseth him [the Father] that sent me."*[129]

And again,

> *". . . no one shall be appointed to receive commandments and revelations in this church excepting my servant . . . for*

127. D&C 107:91–92.
128. D&C 84:88, brackets added.
129. Luke 10:16.

he receiveth them even as Moses.

"And thou shalt be obedient unto the things which I shall give unto him . . .

"For I have given him the keys of the mysteries, and the revelations which are sealed, until I shall appoint unto them another in his stead."[130]

Besides Emmeline Wells, to others, all of them quoted in this study, the Lord's servant—whether the Prophet, Brigham Young, John Taylor, or another, who possessed the mantle of authority and power, who held a fulness of all the keys, was a man "transfigured." In their attempts to describe their witness of this indication of the divine will, they used different words: [Brigham Young] "transfiguration" (Mary Pugh Scott), "look, attitude, dress and appearance . . . the spirit and mantle . . . was upon him" (Benjamin F. Johnson); "the look . . . the voice . . . and . . . the mantle" (Mosiah Lyman Hancock), "spoke with the voice" (John Pulsipher and Zerah Pulsipher), "surely it was his voice and gestures" and everyone "could easily see upon whom the priesthood descended" (Drusilla Hendricks), "how calm and peaceful the spirit and feelings . . . and the words which were uttered came, accompanied by the convincing power of God . . . filled with the Spirit and with great joy" (George Q. Cannon), "the very gestures . . . very features . . . even the stature . . . words went through me like electricity . . . went through me with the thrill of conviction" (Orson Hyde), "power of the Holy Ghost, even the spirit of the prophets" (Brigham Young), "the same voice, the same gestures, the same stature" (Ezra T. Clark), "the mantle . . . as that of Elijah . . .

130. D&C 28:2–7.

upon Elisha . . . voice . . . gestures . . . all . . . again with us" (Nancy Naomi Tracy), "the form, voice and countenance . . . transfigured . . . appeared . . . in every particular" (Benjamin Ashby), "looked very much like . . . so much so that at first sight I thought he was" (Joseph Grafton Hovey), "power and the testimony of the Prophet was in his utterances" (Seymour Bicknell Young), "very appearance, the very voice and manner" (Susa Young Gates and Leah D. Widtsoe), "countenance seemed to change" (Rachel Ridgeway Ivins Grant), "voice and manner became changed" (Henry Shuler Buckwalter), "possessed the mantle" (Ezra Taft Benson), "the mantle . . . was upon him" (William Bryan Pace), "even the different actions or gestures were the same" (Bathsheba W. Smith), "the wonderful and startling effect that it had upon us . . . could hardly have made a deeper or more lasting impression" (Helen Mar Whitney), "spoke with the voice of . . . the Prophet" (Homer Duncan),"I rose to my feet to look . . . because I thought I heard his voice . . . and felt his spirit and the influence that he had" (Robert T. Burton), "a general feeling of relief . . . power and influence . . . rested upon him" (Lyman Littlefield), "visibly saw the mantle . . . that is the voice of the true shepherd" (Jacob Hamblin), "through the gloom could be plainly felt the rod of iron . . . whole being seemed changed . . . wonderful transformation, and . . . the power of that change remained" (Mary Ann Winters), "face illuminated and . . . the divine thrill . . . and the impression" (Jane Snyder Richards), "his face and countenance having the appearance . . . his voice and words were the familiar voice and words . . . the feelings that possessed my breast . . . the countenance, voice and the manner of the speech of the Prophet . . . the mantle of the Prophet" (Lewis Barney), "the mantle . . . the power of God . . . the voice of the shepherd" (Wilford Woodruff), "the spirit and power of the Almighty . . . descended upon the man . . . clothed with such power . . . outpouring of the gift of God upon that man . . . the chosen one . . . the authority, and the power, and the gifts . . . the Lord magnified him" (George Q. Cannon), "darkness was dispelled . . . the voice of the true shepherd . . . great and marvelous was the manner in which the manifestation before the entire congregation was made . . . great relief and joy" (William Lampard Watkins), "God clothed him with the power of presidency . . . perfectly apparent that another leader [John Taylor] had been provided, and that he, from that time, would be the strongest and mightiest man among them" (Orson F. Whitney), and "when we do our duty, when we live our religion, we shall have these principles manifested to us [Wilford Woodruff]" (Wilford Woodruff).

Like those who have gone before, we too may receive a witness that the mantle of the prophets rests upon the leaders of the Church. And like those who have gone before, we will not all use the same words, or phrases, to describe the witness that may come to us. Their framework for comparison focused only upon the Prophet Joseph Smith: did Brigham Young possess the same "mantle," or the same "look" and "gestures" as the Prophet Joseph? Or upon Brigham Young: did John Taylor possess the same "mantle," or the same "power of presidency," or "strength and might" as Brigham Young?

Our frame of reference involves many prophets and many successions, and so we should comprehend that the assurance does not stand on traits of personality, mannerisms and gestures, or elements of demeanor. Over 160 years since that fateful meeting at the Stand, on Thursday, August 8, 1844, we should understand that the assurance comes by the sweet, powerful witness of the Holy Ghost, speaking peace in the quiet chambers of the soul, that the Lord has called the Prophet who stands before us.

Reflection suggests that the Lord's purpose in allowing participation in the protocol of common consent[131] is to provide a forum in which the Saints may receive a witness of His selection and approval of those whom He has called to lead.[132] Not many years ago, Harold B. Lee became the eleventh President of the Church, tenth in succession after the Prophet Joseph Smith. Only a few months before he himself was called to wield the mantle of Presidency following the passing of President Joseph Fielding Smith, Harold B. Lee, in an address presented in General Conference, affirmed:

> *"Someone has said . . . and I believe it to be absolutely true: 'That person is not truly converted until he sees the power of God resting upon the leaders of this church, and it goes down into his heart like fire.' Until the members of this Church have that conviction that . . . these men of God . . . have been properly appointed by the hand of God, they are not truly converted."*[133]

---

131. See footnote #46, #50 above.

132. "We believe that a man must be called of God, by prophecy [that is, by a prophetic declaration—by revelation, from the Lord to the presiding authority], and by the laying on of hands by those who are in authority [after interviews, and confirmation by the Spirit, the call is extended, and accepted, and the candidate is then ordained or set apart, by those who preside], to preach the Gospel and administer in the ordinances thereof," (Articles of Faith 5).

133. President Harold B. Lee, *"Faith in Leadership,"* 142nd Annual Conference, Saturday, April 8, 1972, ***Conference Report***, April 1972, p. 118, italics added.

At the time, the Saints harbored the expectation that President Lee would probably serve for a number of years, because he followed after President Joseph Fielding Smith who served until just two weeks short of his 96th birthday, and President David O. McKay who served until nine months past his 96th birthday. When President Lee died three months before his 75th birthday (Wednesday, December 26, 1973), and because he had served as President of the Church for a period of only eighteen months, many of the Saints were unprepared.

William Grant Bangerter, a member of the First Quorum of the Seventy and Supervisor of the Brazil Area at the time, described an event that occurred a few months later. In an address presented in general conference, he said:

> *"President Harold B. Lee passed away suddenly . . . His death was completely unexpected . . . His leadership . . . nature . . . sound judgment . . . influence and . . . evident spiritual stature . . . commended him to the members of the Church as one of the great men of our time. He possessed an ususal ability to relate as a personal friend to countless people. It was expected that . . . he would preside for . . . years . . .*
>
> *"Suddenly he was gone!—called elsewhere . . . In deep sorrow and concern . . . questions arose in the minds of the people, much as they did at the time when Joseph Smith was killed in Carthage, Illinois. 'What will we do now? How can we carry on . . .'*
>
> *"Of course we knew that the Church would survive . . . We had not thought of Spencer W. Kimball becoming the president . . . We knew . . . that he would manage somehow, but . . . things would not be the same . . .*

". . . gathered that morning [Thursday, April 4, 1974] in the Church Office Building [were] all of the General Authorities as well as the Regional Representatives and other leaders from the around the world. We were to be instructed once again, as we had been periodically during the past seven years. On each preceding occasion Harold B. Lee had given us our direction and sounded the trump of leadership. Now he was no longer there, and we all felt his absence deeply . . .

"The moment came when President Kimball arose to address the assembled leadership. He noted that he also had never expected to occupy this position and that he missed President Lee equally with the rest of us . . .[134]

"As he proceeded with his address, however, he had not spoken very long when a new awareness seemed suddenly to fall on the congregation. We became alert to an astonishing spiritual presence, and we realized that we were listening to something unusual, powerful, different from any of our previous meetings. It was as if, spiritually speaking, our hair began to stand on end. Our minds were suddenly vibrant and marveling at the transcendent message that was coming to our ears. With a new perceptiveness we realized that President Kimball was opening spiritual windows, and beckoning to us to come and gaze with him on the plans of eternity. It was as if he were drawing back the curtains which covered the purposes of the Almighty and inviting us to view with him the destiny

---

134. The address to which Elder Bangerter refers, that President Spencer W. Kimball delivered to the Seminar for Regional Representatives, Thursday, April 4, 1974, was entitled "*When the World Will Be Converted,*" and was published in ***The Ensign***, Vol. 4 (October 1974), pp. 2–6, and printed again, on the 10th anniversary of the month it was first presented, in ***The Ensign***, Vol. 14 (April 1984), pp. 2–6.

of the gospel and the vision of its ministry. I doubt that any person present that day will ever forget the occasion . . .

"The Spirit of the Lord was upon President Kimball and it proceeded from him to us as a tangible presence, which was at once both moving and shocking. He unrolled to our view a glorious vision . . .

"President Kimball spoke under this special influence for an hour and ten minutes. It was a message totally unlike any other in my experience. I realized that it was similar to the occasion on the 8th of August, 1844, when Brigham Young spoke to the Saints in Nauvoo following the death of the Prophet Joseph. Sidney Rigdon had returned from Pittsburgh, where he had apostatized, to try to capture the Church. Many people testified, however, that as Brigham Young arose, the power of the Lord rested upon him to the extent that he was transfigured before them, with the appearance and voice of Joseph Smith. That moment was decisive in the history of the Church, and the occasion of April 4, 1974, is parallel.

"When President Kimball concluded, President Ezra Taft Benson arose and with a voice filled with emotion, echoing the feeling of all present, said, in substance, 'President Kimball, though all the years that these meetings have been held, we have never heard such an address as you have just given. Truly, there is a prophet in Israel.'

"Now I affirm that since April 1974 things have indeed not been the same. This is no attempt to eulogize President Kimball into a figure greater than other presidents of the Church, but to point out the continuing spiritual power which attends the prophet of the Lord, whoever he may be . . ."[135]

135. Elder William Grant Bangerter of the Seventy and President of the Brazil

President Gordon B. Hinckley, at the time a member of the Quorum of the Twelve and ranked sixth in the Quorum, stated: "That was the greatest talk ever given in these seminars . . . None of us can ever be quite the same after that."[136] Later that same day, President Ezra Taft Benson, at the time President of the Quorum of the Twelve, recorded of President Kimball: "The Lord is magnifying him. The mantle of the President has fallen upon him . . ."[137]

President George Q. Cannon,[138] in an address presented on the birthday of the Prophet, in a special meeting convened for the occasion in the Tabernacle in Salt Lake City, Sunday evening, December 23, 1894, reminded the Saints that

> *". . . even when Joseph was slain— probably as dark an hour as the Church ever saw—and when men cast about not knowing where to look and whom to follow, there was in the hearts of the people of God an unshaken faith that the Lord would not leave His people and suffer the work that He had established to be overthrown."*[139]

Area, "*A Special Moment in Church History*," from an address at the Saturday afternoon session of the 147th Semi-annual General Conference, in the Tabernacle in Salt Lake City, Saturday, October 1, 1977, cited in ***The Ensign***, November 1977, pp. 26–27; compare ***Conference Report***, October 1977, pp. 37–40, italics and brackets added. Used by special permission.

136. As cited in Edward L. Kimball and Andrew E. Kimball, Jr., "*The Prophet of the Lord*," ***Spencer W. Kimball: Twelfth President of The Church of Jesus Christ of Latter-day Saints***, 1st Edition (Salt Lake City: Bookcraft, Inc., 1977), p. 416.

137. Thursday, April 4, 1974 . Cited in Sheri L. Dew, "*President of the Twelve*," ***Ezra Taft Benson: A Biography*** (Salt Lake City: Deseret Book Company, 1987), p. 431.

138. See footnotes #120 (biographical sketch), and #23, #25, #40, #52-54, and #66.

139. President George Q. Cannon, at the time First Counselor to President Wilford Woodruff, "*Prophet of the Nineteenth Century*," **Collected Discourses**

And thus it will ever be, "as one passes beyond the veil, following his file leader, the next Apostle will follow after . . . to bear off this kingdom"[140] in all the days ahead, "until He reigns whose right it is to reign,"[141] for, as the Prophet Samuel promised the hosts of Israel ages ago, the ". . . Lord will not forsake His people . . ."[142]

THE END

Delivered by President Wilford Woodruff, His Two Counselors, The Twelve Apostles, and Others, comp., ed. Brian H. Stuy, 5 Volumes (Woodland Hills, Utah: B. H. S. Publishing, 1987–1992), Vol. 4, Sunday, December 23, 1894.

140. Elder Erastus Snow, "*The Quorums of the Priesthood Will Continue to Go Forward— The Saints Are Calm and Undisturbed,*" as reported by Rudger Clawson, in ***Journal of Discourses***, Vol. 19, pp. 102–103, italics added.

141. Revelation to the Prophet Joseph Smith. Between Monday, August 1, and Sunday, August 7, 1831, members of the Colesville Branch from New York and members of the Thompson Branch from Ohio arrived at Zion, Jackson County, Missouri, a meeting was held at which Brother W. W. Phelps preached, and many of the Saints desired to know the will of the Lord concerning them in the new gathering place, in Zion, at Jackson County, Missouri, Monday, August 1, 1831, D&C 58:22.

142. 1 Samuel 12:22.

Bibliography

Adams, William. *"Autobiography 1822–1849."* Typescript, January, 1894. L. Tom Perry Special Collections, Harold B. Lee Library, Brigham Young University.

Ashby, Benjamin. *"Autobiography."* Copy of holograph. L. Tom Perry Special Collections, Harold B. Lee Library, Brigham Young University.

Barney, Lewis. *"Autobiography."* Typescript, L. Tom Perry Special Collections, Harold B. Lee Library, Brigham Young University, Provo, Utah.

Barney, Lewis. "***Reminiscences,***" (ca. 1886–1888). Church Historical Department, Archives Division, Salt Lake City, Utah.

Barney, Ronald O. *"A Brief Chronology of the Life of Lewis Barney (1808–1894)."* Church Historical Department, Archives Division, Salt Lake City, Utah.

Barney, Ronald O. ***One Side By Himself: The Life and Times of Lewis Barney, 1808–1894***. Logan, Utah: Utah State University Press, 2001.

Benson, Ezra Taft. "Autobiography." ***The Juvenile Instructor***. Salt Lake City. 80:213–214 (1945).

Brooke, Henry and Catherine, to Leonard and Mary Pickel, Friday, November 15, 1844. Leonard Pickel Papers. The Frederick W. and Carrie S. Beinecke Library of Western Americana, Yale University, New Haven, Connecticut.

Cannon, George Q. ***The Juvenile Instructor***. 5:174–175, 182 (October 29, 1879).

Collected Discourses. Comp. Ed. Brian H. Stuy. 5 Volumes. Burbank, California and Woodland Hills, Utah. BHS Publishing, 1987–1992. Vol. 5.

Conference Report of The Church of Jesus Christ of Latter-day Saints. October, 1880, 1897–Present.

Contributor Salt Lake City, 1879–1896. 10:336–337 (July 1889).

Diary of Brigham Young (Manuscript History of Brigham Young). Brigham Young Collection. Church Historical Department, Archives Division, Salt Lake City. August 8, 1844.

Gates, Susa Young and Widtsoe, Leah D. ***The Life Story of Brigham Young***. New York: The MacMillan Company, 1930.

Grant, Rachel Ridgeway Ivins. "Joseph Smith," ***The Young Women's Journal***. Salt Lake City. 16:551 (1905).

Hamblin, Jacob. ***A Narrative of His Personal Experience as a Frontiersman, Missionary to the Indians, and Explorer—Disclosing Interpositions of Providence, Severe Privations, Perilous Situations and Remarkable Escapes,*** Narrated to and Edited by James A. Little, 2nd Edition. Salt Lake City: Deseret News, 1909.

Hancock, Mosiah Lyman. "*Life Story of Mosiah Lyman Hancock.*" Typescript, 1965. L. Tom Perry Special Collections, Harold B. Lee Library, Brigham Young University.

Hendricks, Drusilla. "*Historical Sketch.*" Church Historical Department, Archives Division,, Salt Lake City.

Improvement Era. Salt Lake City, 1897–1970. 5:200–202 (January, 1902); 21: 752–753 (June 1918).

Jenson, Andrew. ***The Historical Record***. 4 Volumes. Salt Lake City: The Andrew Jenson Publishing Company, 1887.

Johnson, Benjamin F. ***My Life's Review***. Independence, Missouri: Zion's Printing and Publishing Company, 1928.

Journal of Wilford Woodruff. Wilford Woodruff Collection. Church Historical Department, Archives Division,, Salt Lake City. August 7–8, 1844.

Juvenile Instructor, The. Salt Lake City, 1866–1929. 22:174–175 (October 29, 1879).

Littlefield, Lyman O. ***Reminiscences of Latter-day Saints***. Logan, Utah: The Utah Journal Company, 1888. Chapter 2.

Laub, George. ***The Journal of George Laub 1814–1846***. Church Historical Department, Archives Division, Salt Lake City, Utah.

Madsen, Carol Cornwall. ***Journey to Zion: Voices from the Mormon Trail***. Salt Lake City, Utah: Deseret Book Company, 1997.

Manuscript History of Brigham Young, Church Historical Department, Archives Division,, Salt Lake City, Utah.

Millennial Star, The. Manchester, Liverpool and London, England. 1840–1970. 25:216 (1865).

Morris, George. "*Autobiography*." Typescript, L. Tom Perry Special Collections, Harold B. Lee Library, Brigham Young University.

Mouritsen, Robert G. ***The Office of Associate President of The Church of Jesus Christ of Latter-day Saints***. Master's Thesis, n.p., 1972. Department of Church History and Doctrine, Brigham Young University. L. Tom Perry Special Collections, Harold B. Lee Library, Brigham Young University, Provo, Utah.

Mouritsen, Robert G. "*Windy Day in August, at Nauvoo: When the Mantle of the Prophet Joseph Smith Fell Upon Brigham Young, and He was Sustained as Leader of the Church According to the Doctrine of Apostolic Succession*." Paper for Graduate Religion, n.p., 1974. L. Tom Perry Special Collections, Harold B. Lee Library, Brigham Young University, Provo, Utah.

Pace, William Bryan. "*Autobiography*." Typescript, L. Tom Perry Special Collections, Harold B. Lee Library, Brigham Young University.

Pratt, Parley P. ***Autobiography of Parley P. Pratt***. Ed. Parley Parker Pratt. 4th Edition Salt Lake City: Deseret Book Company, 1950.

Pulsipher, John. "*Autobiography*." Typescript. L. Tom Perry Special Collections, Harold B. Lee Library, Brigham Young University.

Pulsipher, Zerah. "*Autobiography*." Typescript. L. Tom Perry Special Collections, Harold B. Lee Library, Brigham Young University.

Rich, Russell R. ***Those Who Would Be Leaders***. Provo, Utah: Brigham Young University Press, 1967.

Richards, Jane Snyder. "*Joseph Smith*." ***The Young Women's Journal***. 16:550 (1905).

Roberts, Brigham Henry. ***Comprehensive History of the Church***. 6 Volumes. Exact Lithographic Reprint of 1930 Edition. Provo, Utah: Brigham Young University Press, 1965. Vol. 2.

Roberts, Brigham Henry. ***The Rise and Fall of Nauvoo***. Salt Lake City: Deseret News Press, 1960. Exact lithographic reproduction of original, Salt Lake City: Bookcraft, 1965.

Romney, George. "*A Testimony*," ***The Improvement Era***. 21:752–753 (June 1918).

Scott, Mary Pugh. "*Life Story of Mary Pugh [Scott]*," 1848, typescript copy. Utah State Historical Society Archives, Salt Lake City, Utah.

"*Selecting, Sustaining, Ordaining and Setting Apart a New President of the Church*." ***The Improvement Era***. Salt Lake City, 1897–1970. 59:528 (July, 1956).

Smith, Joseph. ***Doctrine and Covenants***. Enlarged Format Edition with LDS Scripture References. Salt Lake City and London: The Church of Jesus Christ of Latter-day Saints, 1985.

Smith, Joseph. ***A History of The Church of Jesus Christ of Latter-day Saints***. Edited by B. H. Roberts. 7 Vols. 2nd ed. rev. Salt Lake City: Brigham Young University Press, 1965–1970.

Smith, Joseph. ***The Teachings of the Prophet Joseph Smith***. Compiled by President Joseph Fielding Smith. 2nd Printing of Edition with Index by Dr. Robert J. Matthews. Salt Lake City: Deseret Book Company, 1985.

Smith, Joseph Fielding, President. ***Doctrines of Salvation***. Compiled and Edited by Elder Bruce R. McConkie. 3 Volumes. 24th Printing. Salt Lake City: Bookcraft, Inc., 1990. Vol. 1 and 2.

Smith, Joseph Fielding. "*Forward*" to Pearson Corbett ***Hyrum Smith: Patriarch***. Salt Lake City: Deseret Book Company, 1963.

Times and Seasons. Nauvoo, Illinois. Volumes 5 and 6.

Tracy, Nancy Naomi Alexander. "*Nancy Naomi Alexander Tracy Autobiography*." Typescript. Mormon Collections. Bancroft Library. University of California at Berkeley.

Tracy, Nancy Naomi Alexander. "*Autobiography*." Typescript. L. Tom Perry Special Collections. Harold B. Lee Library. Brigham Young University.

Watkins, William Lampard. "*Autobiography 1827–1846*." Typescript. L. Tom Perry Special Collections, Harold B. Lee Library, Brigham Young University.

Watson, Eldon J., comp. Manuscript History of Brigham Young, 1801–1844. Salt Lake City: Smith Secretarial Service, 1968.

Whitney, Helen Mar Kimball. "*Scenes in Nauvoo*." ***Woman's Exponent***. Salt Lake City. 11:129–131 (1882).

Winters, Mary Ann Sterns. "*Autobiography*." Typescript. Church Historical Department, Archives Division,, Salt Lake City.

Young, Brigham, et. al. ***Journal of Discourses***, ed. George D. Watt, et al., originally published in Liverpool, England, by Franklin D. Richards, et. al., 26 Volumes. London: Latter-day Saint Book Depot, 1854–1886), 5th exact lithographic reprint of original edition (Salt Lake City, 1978).

Young Woman's Journal. Salt Lake City, 1889–1929. 16:550–551, 554–555 (1905).

Index